THE VINTAGE WORKSHOP
Art-to-Wear

100 Images & 40 Projects to Personalize Fashion

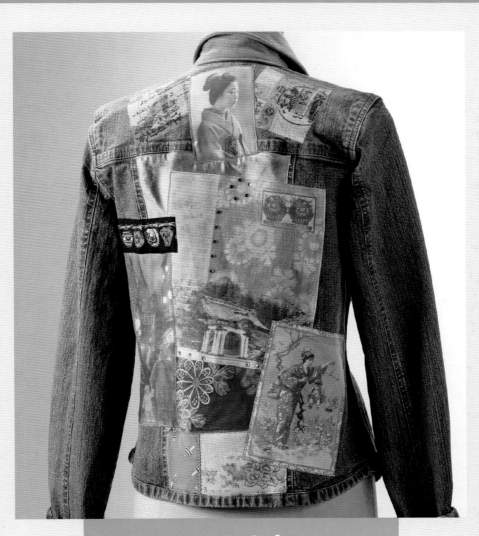

Amy Barickman

The Vintage Workshop Art-to-Wear: 100 Images & 40 Projects to Personalize Fashion
copyright ©2006 by The Vintage Workshop

"Come & Get It" artwork page 50, © Connie Ehrich
Halloween Fairy Collage artwork page 104, © Chris Farr

Publisher: Amy Marson
Editorial Director: Gailen Runge
Acquisitions Editor: Jan Grigsby
Editor: Amy Barickman/Jean Lowe
Technical Editor: Deb Rowden
Copyeditor: Deb Rowden

Proofreader: Jean Lowe
Cover Designer: Desiree Mueller
Book Designer: Desiree Mueller
Photo Stylist: Kayte Price
Photography by Chris Dennis Photography

Published by C&T Publishing, Inc., P.O. Box 1456, Lafayette, CA 94549

Library of Congress Cataloging-in-Publication Data

Barickman, Amy
  The vintage workshop art-to-wear : 100 images & 40 projects to personalize fashion / Amy Barickman.
     p. cm.
  ISBN-13: 978-1-57120-388-5 (paper trade : alk. paper)
  ISBN-10: 1-57120-388-5 (paper trade : alk. paper)
  1. Handicraft. 2. Transfer-printing. 3. Iron-on transfers. I. Title.

  TT880.B2965 2006
  746.6'2--dc22

                              2006010335

Printed in China   10 9 8 7 6 5 4 3 2 1

Please note that the use of soldering equipment is an inherently dangerous activity and that by engaging in this hobby, you are assuming the risk of injury including, without limitation, injuries associated with exploding glass and heat burns.

Dedication

*This book is dedicated to graphic artists and illustrators from years gone by—
those many forgotten or unidentified talents who created the charming
artwork that is found in The Vintage Workshop's creative offering.
May this book excite and inspire others in future generations.*

Acknowledgments

When I was just a child, my mother and grandmother taught me to love and
appreciate old fabrics, laces, photographs and art. They inspired me to start a business
using them, thus, The Vintage Workshop began.

Jean Lowe helped grow The Vintage Workshop by introducing product licensing.
She has managed this entire book project—its design, editorial and production. Without
Jean this book would not have happened.

Kayte Price is the photo stylist for the book. Her tireless efforts in creative
direction have brought creativity and style to The Vintage Workshop and Indygo
Junction product lines.

Desiree Mueller is lead designer and graphics coordinator for the book. She
has also contributed her talents designing collaged art .

An awesome designer of many projects—clothing and beyond—for this publi-
cation, Mary Ann Donze's incredible talent contributes to the success of The Vintage
Workshop and Indygo Junction. Her projects appear on pages 16, 19, 23, 25, 26, 27,
28, 31, 46, 54, 74, 77, 78, 83 and 84.

Designer Tamara Vandergriff added a whimsical style to our wearable projects
with beading and embroidery and paid careful attention to every detail. Tamara's
creations are on pages 58, 59, 106, 107, 108, 109, 111, 112, 113, and 114.

Tommi Ringle expanded the possibilities for material in this book by creating
our soldered jewelry collection with beautiful craftsmanship and unique style. Her
jewelry appears on pages 87, 88, 105 and 111.

Delsie Chambon is a creator of collaged art for The Vintage Workshop.

Special thanks to publisher Amy Marson and her team at C&T Publishing.

Contents

 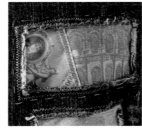

CONTENTS
Art-to-Wear

CHAPTER 5

About the Author

Amy Barickman, founder and owner of Indygo Junction, Inc., and The Vintage Workshop, grew up in the retail crafting business and is today a leader in the quilt and clothing pattern craft industry. She started Indygo Junction in 1990 to showcase the talent of leading craft designers. Amy's knack for anticipating popular styles and trends has helped her discover and mentor fresh, new design talent. To date, she has worked with more than 25 artists, guiding them, through a unique partnership, to create with innovative materials.

She began The Vintage Workshop in 2002 to create products that combine the timeless beauty of vintage artwork with the remarkable accessibility of the computer and inkjet printable materials. In *The Vintage Workshop Art-to-Wear*, Amy has once again brought together her own skills with those of other talented designers to create a great collection of projects for every level of crafter. The result is a collection that showcases The Vintage Workshop's timeless images and creative inspirations.

See her other new book, *Indygo Junction's Needle Felting*, in which Amy introduces another fabulous crafting technique with projects that are both stylish and sophisticated.

Introduction
What is Art-to-Wear?

The trend in clothing and crafting is for personalization. Go to any retail store these days, and it's obvious that people are looking for unique fashions that are one-of-kind and personalized. Even mass market retailers are trying to bring original embellishments to fashion and accessories, giving them the feel of originality with the addition of beads, sequins, monograms, and hand stitching.

At The Vintage Workshop, we are all about using what's old to make it new again. I have collected, and in some cases collaged, thousands of images that I have found by scouring flea markets and antique stores. Over the years, I have scanned and stored these images as digital files. The Vintage Workshop has led the way in using technology—

that is, our home computers, scanners, and printers—to print these images to fabrics that are made specifically for inkjet printing. We have also developed a line of fabrics that are manufactured for use in crafts and fashion.

The most common fabric that our designers use is cotton poplin. Other fabrics that are

available include canvas and silk. By clicking on the artwork you wish to use on the enclosed CD, you can directly print that image to a fabric sheet that can be ironed, sewn, or embellished to create awesome and one-of-a-kind fashions. We will show you here how to do it.

I can hear you saying, "but technology isn't in my experience." That's okay, too, because in this book we also give you the images printed on quality four-color pages throughout. At the end of each chapter, you'll find a reproduction of the images used in that chapter. This allows you to also use a color copier so you can reproduce the image directly to any material you choose.

I am excited to show you some of the exceptional creations we've designed with images that are vintage, retro, and original— but always with a contemporary flair. Why pay designer prices for fashions you can create on your own, making your "art-to-wear," truly one-of-a-kind?

Amy Barickman

How to Use This Book

The designers at The Vintage Workshop, who created these fashions, brought their own unique style and flair to the projects. They try to use fabrics, patterns, and trims that are readily available and accessible to everyone. Since our workshop also tries to take the best of our vintage collection and make it new again, you will also see some one-of-a-kind embellishments on some of the fashions. We encourage you to use your own collection of vintage trims, trinkets, buttons, ephemera, fabric swatches, and paper.

When we use a specific product, we list it in the Supplies list with the instructions. Following each chapter, you will find the images used on those project. We also list the images that were used on the project instructions page. That way, you can go right to that image on the disc, click, and print. You are also welcome to use any of the other images as substitutes for what our designers have used. Part of the fun of learning to use digital technology in crafting is the ease with which you can actually create your own personalized style.

If you decided to substitute different artwork on your project, keep in mind that the dimensions may vary and you will need to adjust accordingly. Depending on the the size of the garment you are embellishing you may want to consider adjusting the size of the image before printing. We have provided high resolution jpegs on the CD for each image. These images can be easily resized in many word processing or design image editing programs. You can do as many of the individual steps as you like on each piece and even mix and match these ideas from other projects as well.

Another bonus is the fact that you have access to the images in the book itself. With a multitude of unique printable materials now available, you can color-copy or print the images and use them in other ways, on other projects, for scrapbooking, paper crafts, and home décor—the possibilities are endless.

Printing Images

All of the images used in the projects in this book are available on the CD packaged with this book. They have been sized and placed in the chapters in which they appear. After inserting the CD in your computer system, an opening screen will appear on which you can view the chapters of the book.

When you open the Chapter screen, a gallery of the images from that chapter will be available that are pre-sized in PDF format for each project. Simply click on the page icon that matches the project you're working on. The PDFs will be 8 ½" x 11" in size, ranging from one to several pages long. Depending on your computer, choose the print icon on your tool bar. The image will print to size and no adjustments are necessary. The CD also provides jpeg files for each image in folders arranged by chapter. These files allow you greater flexibility for sizing and cropping the images to meet your specific needs.

Inkjet Printable Materials

Inkjet Printables:

The Vintage Workshop also specializes in using inkjet printable fabrics—in fact, we offer a full range of products that we have tested and produced for use on our projects. You can visit our website to view a full collection of our fabrics, papers, and transfers and order materials directly from us, if you desire. Most materials used in this book are also readily available at crafts stores.

For best results, you should store your material in a low-humidity area, since it can be affected by moisture. You should also store your inkjet fabric flat, between protective cardboard or in a bag. Its finish is durable and it can be handled without fear of leaving marks on it.

Always read the product directions before you print the fabric. Once you get the hang of working with these fabrics, they require very little in the way of preparation. Most of these materials come with a paper backing. This aids in feeding the materials through the printer with more ease. Before you load the sheet onto the printer—and we recommend only feeding one sheet at a time into your carriage—look for frayed or loose ends. Trim these away from the sheet before loading. Also, make sure you have the correct side running face-up in your printer. Test-run the image first on plain paper, to be sure you have the ink level you need and the correct image.

Once you print the image on the fabric, simply peel off the backing to release the fabric. Many of the inkjet fabrics are colorfast. The Vintage Workshop designers have not encountered any difficulties, but just in case, we always take a few precautions. It's best to hand wash or dry-clean your finished projects. For extra durability, waterproofing, and colorfastness, you may spray the images with clear acrylic finish. We often recommend Krylon NO. 1303.

Inkjet Transfers:

The transfers we recommend and offer are Iron-on products that offer a "no-fail" direct transfer application. There is no mirroring of an image required. Simply print the image to the "right side" material, cut it out exactly to the edge of the design, and peel off the paper backing. Place the transfer material right side up on the wearable, cover with the reusable parchment-like silicon pressing sheet included in the package and iron in place according to the manufacturer's instructions. Wait for the garment to cool before removing the silicon sheet. You will be pleased with the rich color, satin-type finish you will achieve with these transfers. The Vintage Workshop's Iron-on II is opaque and recommended for light or dark colored fabrics. Iron-on II is also your best choice for a rough texture, like canvas or denim. Iron-on I is also the direct transfer process explained above, but is translucent and recommended for white and light fabrics. This transfer will have some show through of the color of the garment it is applied to, and also has a matte finish. Both transfers offer the ability to layer one on top of the other for unique effects. We've even experimented with great success adding iron-on crystals to our transfers and fabrics.

A Word about Adhesives and Tools

A variety of adhesive materials are also available at crafts stores. This list would include fusible webbing, glue sticks, spray mount adhesives and hot-glue guns, to name a few. Always follow the manufacturer's recommendations. In our Supplies list and instructions, we tell you what we used to make our finished piece. Many, if not most of our projects use iron-on transfers, and fabrics that are then hand-embellished or sewn.

We also list the tools you will need to identify before you begin the project. You probably have most of the tools on hand for sewing and crafting. Check over our lists before you begin for any unusual items that the project designer used.

Now have fun, be creative, and feel free to write or send us your inspired creations! We promise you won't see your outfit coming and going!

General Directions for Preparing Images

Depending on the inkjet fabric you use in a project, a rinsing step may be suggested. After printing desired images, rinse them swiftly under cold running water, being careful not to let the image fold back over itself. This process removes any excess ink. Lay flat or hang to dry. They dry quickly and may be ironed if necessary before use. In all project directions, it is assumed that this step has already been taken unless specified otherwise. Remember that you need not use the ENTIRE image. It is fun to crop the image and use only sections at times.

Wearables for Children

What joy there is in making baby and children's clothing! And what a wonderful collection of images, both vintage and modern, are available for personalizing your projects. Why pay designer prices for clothing that can be made at a fraction of the cost? It is so much fun to use your own imagination to embellish these projects. I think we have chosen some interesting starting points to get your creative juices flowing. Don't limit yourself—rummage through your vintage buttons and fabrics. When the child outgrows these clothes, you'll want to keep them as a keepsake and memory of these happy times.

Clover Girl Romper

Any basic romper pattern will work for this darling garment. We suggest one constructed with a center seam so that you can showcase four fabulous fabrics for a fun and funky look. Our sample uses four great vintage barkcloth pieces. Little girls have been known to love the giant pom poms too! With the charming vintage photograph, the delicate rickrack, and fun palette of fabrics, any child will look delightful in this comfortable creation.

SUPPLIES:

- 1 sheet of The Vintage Workshop Cotton Poplin
- Clover Girl image (printed size approximately 3 ½" x 5")
- Pattern for girl's romper with center front and back seams
- Five lengths of fabric, vintage or new. One will be for facing. The other four will be for each of the four sections of the romper.
- ½ yd. or more small black rickrack
- Two ¾" buttons, vintage or new
- 1 yd. or more of large black pom poms
- Sewing thread for garment
- Black thread for rickrack
- Dritz Fray Check™

INSTRUCTIONS:

When cutting out romper, use a different fabric for each section and facing.

1. Stitch together romper front according to pattern directions.

2. Cut out the image with a ½" border. Press under ½" all around and pin to upper front, centered over seam. Stitch close to folded edge.

3. Stitch black rickrack around image, centered over folded edge.

4. Complete garment as directed except hem.

5. Finish lower legs of romper with serging. Turn under ⅝" and pin.

6. Beginning at inner leg seam, slide pom pom yardage under hem so that only the pom poms are exposed. Trim at required length. Pin again through pom pom tape and stitch around leg close to lower edge. Stitch again ¼" from first stitching. Apply Dritz Fray Check™ to cut ends of pom pom tape.

This can be adapted to any romper pattern, preferably one with center seams and a cargo pocket. A regular pocket will also work. The vintage plaid fabric used as a complement to the coordinating images may be printed from the CD or copied from the image pages. We show this romper constructed from two red cottons with subtle patterns, with vintage buttons to keep it fastened. A boy and his dog, chasing a red balloon, equals happiness.

Boy's Balloon Romper

INSTRUCTIONS:

1. Construct pocket according to pattern directions for right leg of romper. Cut a piece of vintage plaid the height of finished pocket plus 1" x 3 ¼". Turn long sides under ¼" and press. Turn lower edge under ½" and press. Turn top edge under ½" and press. Slide this ½" over top edge of pocket and pin. Stitch close to all edges.

2. Cut from canvas the Dog with Purple Balloon image about 1 ¾" wide. Add a ¼" border all around. Press under this border. Center on plaid ⅜" from pocket lower edge and pin. Use a zigzag stitch around image to secure.

3. Stitch **right** front to **right** back at side seam. Center pocket over seam and stitch in place.

4. Stitch **right** front to **left** front. Cut Vintage Plaid piece 5 ¼" x 5 ⅝". Press under ¼" on each side and press. Center over front seam. Pin. Stitch close to edges. **Be sure to leave room for seam allowance to add facing.**

5. Cut Red Balloon image from canvas with a ¼" border. Press under border on each side. Pin to center of plaid. Stitch close to folded edges.

6. Finish construction of garment.

Optional back treatment for romper

1. After left and right back are stitched together, cut a piece of vintage plaid 3 ⅝" x 3 ¾". Turn under each edge ¼" and press. Center over back seam at least 1 ½" down to allow for seam allowance. Pin. Stitch close to folded edges.

2. Print coordinating image of Boy with Purple Balloon on canvas or cotton. Cut from fabric with a ¼" border. This will make it about 2 ⅛" x 2 ¾". Turn under ¼" on edges and press. Center on plaid. Pin. Stitch close to edges.

3. Finish construction of garment.

SUPPLIES:

- **1 sheet of The Vintage Workshop Cotton Canvas**
- **2 sheets of The Vintage Workshop Cotton Poplin**
- **Red Balloon image printed on the cotton canvas (size is approximately 3 ⅞" x 4 ⅝")**
- **Dog with Purple Balloon image printed on the cotton canvas (size is approximately 1 ¾" wide)**
- **Vintage Plaid printed on the cotton poplin**
- **Pattern for boy's romper with center front and back seams, preferably with a cargo pocket**
- **Yardage of two fabrics. The right side, straps, facing and lower pocket will be one fabric. The left side and upper pocket will be a second fabric.**
- **Two ¾" buttons, vintage or new**
- **Thread for garment: green to match plaid, white for images**

Baby T's

Personalized t-shirts are all the craze right now. Why not welcome your new little one—or a friend's new baby—into the world with a customized t-shirt or bib? They are so easy to make with our Iron-on Transfer sheets. Don't be afraid to add your own unique embellishments!

SUPPLIES:

Bath Time T

- **1 sheet The Vintage Workshop Iron-on Transfer II**
- **Bathtime image (printed size approx. 4 ⅛" wide)**
- **1 baby t-shirt, pre-washed**
- **Decorative edge or pinking scissors or craft knife and cutting mat**

Breakfast Time Bib

- **1 sheet The Vintage Workshop Iron-on Transfer II**
- **Clock image (printed size approx. 2 ¾" wide)**
- **1 cloth baby bib, pre-washed**
- **Decorative edge or pinking scissors or craft knife and cutting mat**

Rooster & Rabbit T

- **1 sheet The Vintage Workshop Cotton Poplin Fabric Sheet**
- **Rabbit & Chicks image (printed size approx. 3 ⅜" wide)**
- **1 baby t-shirt, pre-washed**
- **Fusible webbing**
- **Thread**
- **Sewing machine or needle and thread**
- **Scissors or craft knife and cutting mat**

INSTRUCTIONS:

Bath Time T-shirt

1. From the CD, print the Bathtime image.

2. Using scissors or a craft knife, cut images out exactly around the edges.

3. Carefully remove the paper backing from the images and center the image 1 ½" from top edge of shirt. Iron in place following manufacturer's instructions.

Breakfast Time Bib

1. From the CD, print the Clock image.

2. Using scissors or a craft knife, cut images out exactly around the edges.

3. Carefully remove the paper backing from the images and center the image 1 ½" from top edge of the bib. Iron in place following manufacturer's instructions.

Rooster and Rabbit T-shirt

1. From the CD, print the Rabbit & Chicks image to the inkjet fabric sheet, following manufacturer's instructions. Trim the image ¼" from the outer edges.

2. Remove the paper backing from the image. Fuse the image to the paper-backed iron-on adhesive sheet following manufacturer's instructions. Cut the image out exactly around the edges.

3. Remove the paper backing from the image. Center the image approximately 1 ½" to 2" below neckline and fuse it in place following manufacturer's instructions.

4. Stitch around the edges of the image with a zig-zag stitch or stitch in place by hand.

How do I please the princess? May we suggest the Butterfly Girl Dress. It offers an ethereal image encased in thread-wrapped tulle with a pink t-shirt bodice. A few sequins and delicate gold beads never hurt either. To close the deal, a gathered skirt shows off a vintage, floral hankie—folded, pleated, and secured with three sparkling antique glass buttons. Aahhh!!

SUPPLIES:

- **1 sheet The Vintage Workshop Cotton Poplin**
- **One Butterfly Girl image (printed size is approx. 6" x 3 ⅞")**
- **One pink cotton t-shirt**
- **Cotton yardage for skirt**
- **One handkerchief, vintage or reproduction**
- **Three ½" to ⅝" buttons, vintage or new**
- **¼ yard fine black tulle**
- **¼ yard fine pale pink tulle**
- **Iridescent sequins**
- **Gold seed beads**
- **Embroidery floss: dark rose and dusty aqua**
- **Embroidery needle**
- **Beading needle**
- **Sewing thread**
- **Lite Steam-a-Seam® sheet**

Butterfly Girl Dress

INSTRUCTIONS:

1. Cut image from fabric to desired size. No border is necessary.

2. Place the image on the upper chest of the t-shirt where desired. Mark 1 ⅞" **beneath** the lower edge of the image. Cut horizontally across the t-shirt at this marking. This allows a ⅝" seam allowance for attaching the skirt. Discard the lower t-shirt.

3. Following the manufacturer's directions, apply Lite Steam-a-Seam® to the back of image and adhere it to t-shirt in desired spot.

4. On each set of image wings, randomly stitch on 6 or more sequins with a gold bead in the center. Secure the thread at multiple points.

5. Cut 4 lengths of black tulle 7 ¾" x 1". (Adjust the tulle length if image is a different size than 6" x 3 ⅞".) Cut 4 lengths of black tulle 5 ½"x 1 ¼". These need not be cut perfectly straight!

6. Stack 2 of the longer lengths and center them on the top edge of the image. Stack and center the remaining 2 tulle strips on the lower edge of the image. Machine stitch through center of each lengthwise, beginning and ending at image edge.

7. Repeat this with the shorter tulle sections on the **sides** of the image.

8. Cut two 8" lengths of pink tulle about 3" wide. Form into "ropes" and pin one across center of the top black tulle and one across the center of the lower black tulle. Cut two 6" x 3" pink tulle strips. Form into "ropes" and pin to center of side black tulle sections.

9. Cut a fairly long length of the dusty aqua floss and wrap the top and bottom pink tulle ropes about every 1" to 1 ½". Wrap twice at each point and go through shirt beneath to secure. Tie off at ends of image. Cut an ample length of your dark rose floss and repeat this process on the side pink tulle ropes.

10. Trim loose ends of tulle as desired.

11. Determine the desired length of your skirt. Add 2" for the hem and ⅝" for seam allowance. Cut 2 widths of fabric 1 ½ to 2 times the width of your lower shirt.

12. With RST*, stitch ⅝" seams on the sides of the skirt. Press seams open. Gather the upper edge. With RST, pin the skirt to the lower edge of the t-shirt. Stitch together with a ⅝" seam. Trim seam, turn, press and hem.

13. Fold 2 ½" of the top of your handkerchief to the **right** side. Press. Form 2 pleats in the hankie—one near each side. Adjust the depth of the pleats so the hankie fits nicely across the front of the dress. Center the hankie with the folded top just over the seam line. Pin. Sew a button through each pleat to secure and one button in the center. Add additional buttons if you desire.

*RST = right sides together

This unique dress comes equipped with its own pocket purse. That's right! An embellished bag to keep treasures close at hand . . . buttoned to your dress. Piecing this skirt is easy, we promise. Print the vintage fabrics from the CD or use your own. The long sleeved t-shirt bodice is soft and cozy and sports an oh-so-charming silhouette. When the silhouette is covered with black netting, it lends an air of mystery.

SUPPLIES

- 2 sheets The Vintage Workshop Cotton Poplin
- 2 Play Silhouette images approximately 6" x 4" printed on cotton poplin (one for optional pocket purse)
- ¼ yard black netting (not tulle)
- One white cotton t-shirt, long or short sleeved
- 4 fabrics—¼ yard of each
- Lite Steam-a-Seam® sheet
- White thread
- Contrasting thread (blue used on sample)

OPTIONAL POCKET PURSE:

- 4 fabric tabs (see pattern at right)
- Two ⅝" buttons, vintage or new
- 2 fabric and 2 lining pocket pieces measuring 4 ¼" x 4 ½"

Patchwork Silhouette Dress

INSTRUCTIONS:

1. Cut one image from poplin (no border is necessary). Place the image on the upper chest of the t-shirt where desired. Mark 1 ⅞" **beneath** the lower edge of the image. Cut across t-shirt horizontally at this marking. This allows a ⅝" seam allowance for attaching the skirt. Discard the lower t-shirt.

2. Following the manufacturer's directions, apply Lite Steam-a-Seam® to the back of the image and adhere to t-shirt in the desired spot.

3. Cut and center a 7" x 5" piece of black netting over the image. Pin.

4. With contrasting thread, stitch around the edge of the image and through the netting with a zigzag stitch. Trim netting to about ½" beyond the stitching on all sides.

5. To construct the skirt, follow these basic directions: cut out a 4 ½" square piece of paper to use as a pattern. With this pattern, cut 10 squares of each of the 4 fabrics. With these, you will stitch 10 "blocks" comprised of 4 squares each. Decide on the placement of fabrics for your block. With RST*, stitch together 2 of the squares using a ¼" seam. Do not press the seam open. Stitch together the remaining 2 squares. With RST, stitch the first 2 squares to the second two. Press seam

allowances to one side. This is your first block. The dress shown uses 10 identical blocks.

6. With RST, stitch 5 of these blocks together using ¼" seams, alternating fabrics to make one 40 ½" length. Stitch together the remaining 5 blocks in the same manner.

7. With RST, stitch these 2 long sections together along **long** side using a ¼" seam.

8. With RST, stitch the short ends of this completed "quilt" together using ¼" seams. Press. Turn. Gather the upper edge with a basting stitch.

9. With RST, pin skirt to lower edge of shirt, pulling up basting threads to fit. Stitch using a ⅝" seam. Trim and turn. Press. Hem the skirt. Our sample has a 1" hem.

Optional pocket purse instructions:

1. Crop the remaining silhouette image to 2" x 2 ¼". Apply Lite Steam-a-Seam® to the back and iron it to the lower left quadrant of the purse front. Make sure the image is not too close to the seam allowance. Cut a 2 ½" x 2 ¾" piece of black netting. Center it over the image. Zigzag around the image and through the netting with contrasting thread (blue).

2. With RST, stitch pocket purse sides and lower edge using a ¼" seam. Trim corners, turn and press.

3. Place 2 tabs RST. Leaving the straight end open, stitch using a ¼" seam. Trim, turn and press. Stitch a buttonhole on the curved end (see pattern for placement). With RST, align open ends of tabs along the top edge of pocket **back**. Baste tabs in place close to purse edges.

4. With RST, stitch lining pieces together using a ¼" seam, leaving top open and an opening along one side to turn. With RST, pin lining to the pocket and stitch together in ¼" seam. Turn. Slipstitch the side opening closed. Press.

5. Sew buttons on the **right** side of the dress, just below the seam to fit under the pocket purse buttonholes. Button the pocket purse in place.

*RST = right sides together

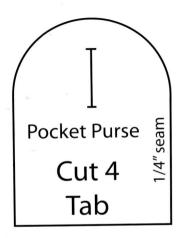

Pocket Purse

Cut 4

Tab

¼" seam

Coloring Fun Smock

This charming and functional smock is a breeze to sew in sturdy denim, to aid your little ones in their creative endeavors. Leave off the buttons and it is suitable for boys to wear during messy activities. The colorful image is appealing to children a nd it is easy for them to put it on themselves. The pocket compartments are great for holding important art supplies or treasures while they have some "coloring fun"!

SUPPLIES:

- 1 sheet The Vintage Workshop Cotton Poplin

- Coloring Fun image printed on cotton poplin as shown, 5 ¼" x 6 ½"

- Stylish Smock IJ730 pattern by Indygo Junction, Inc.

- Yardage of 2 light-weight denims for smock and lining

- Thread to match *lining*, to contrast with smock denim

- 8 vintage or new mismatched buttons of various sizes

- Steam-a-Seam® sheet

INSTRUCTIONS:

1. Follow the pattern instructions to apply the pocket to the smock front. Sew on the 8 assorted buttons across the top of pocket.

2. Cut out the fabric Coloring Fun image with no border. Apply Steam-a-Seam® to the image back according to manufacturer's directions. Center the image on the smock front, 1 ¼" below the neckline. Iron in place. With contrasting thread, stitch with a heavy blanket stitch around all 4 sides of image. If you don't have this stitch on your machine, use a wide zigzag stitch instead.

3. Complete the smock as directed.

Little Chef's Apron

With this cute apron to wear, your child will be eager to help in the kitchen or to just pretend. Have fun choosing contrasting fabrics for the smock and lining. The image used works well with many of the great vintage reproduction fabrics available today. Make a coordinating one for you from the Stylish Smock pattern, and delight your daughter or granddaughter.

INSTRUCTIONS:

1. Cut pocket from Multicolor Mums poplin. Stitch as directed to smock front.

2. Cut a piece of Multicolor Mums fabric 6 ¼" x 8 ¼". Press under ¼" on each edge. Center and pin to the upper front 1" below neckline. Stitch around the edges using a blanket stitch to attach.

3. Cut out the fabric Girl Cook image with no border. Crop slightly to 5" x 6 ½".

4. Apply Steam-a-Seam® to the back of the image according to manufacturer's directions. Iron the image on the center of the black floral. Stitch it in place around all sides using a blanket stitch.

5. Complete the smock following the pattern instructions.

SUPPLIES:

- 1 sheet The Vintage Workshop Cotton Canvas
- 2 sheets The Vintage Workshop Cotton Poplin
- Full page Multicolor Mums image printed on poplin
- Girl Cook image printed on canvas (size is approximately 5" x 7")
- Stylish Smock IJ730 pattern by Indygo Junction, Inc.
- Yardage of 2 cottons for smock and lining
- Thread
- Steam-a-Seam® sheet

SUPPLIES:

- 2 sheets The Vintage Workshop Cotton Poplin
- 1 sheet The Vintage Workshop Cotton Canvas
- 2 sheets The Vintage Workshop Linen
- 1 sheet The Vintage Workshop Iron-On Transfer I
- Denim jean jacket (traditional styling)
- Fabric, trim, and interfacing (if necessary) for collar
- 1 yard of pom poms to fit lower edge of jacket
- One package of ⅛" opening eyelets
- 6 vintage or new shell buttons for collar
- Assorted small scraps of interesting fabrics such as silks, sheers, vintage, etc.
- Embroidery floss in pink & blue; needle
- Denim sewing machine needle
- Small lace and wool scraps (optional)
- 3 vintage or new buttons for front embellishment (silver used on sample)
- Lite Steam-a-Seam® sheet
- 3 or 4 colors of thread for contrast stitching
- Denim color thread
- Pinking sheers
- Seam ripper

This jacket radiates feminine grace with deconstructed elements to add a modern edge. Any girl--child or woman--will stand out in this garment blooming with a bohemian and botanical flair. Vintage images, softly washed with time, are paired with a crisp Japanese text on the back. A new collar is born from vintage floral barkcloth, adorned with a row of time-worn shell buttons at the neck. The sleeves are cleverly reconstructed with insets of vintage images and fabrics. Metal eyelets at the cuffs proclaim a modern look, while hand-sewn trim along the band exudes hand-made charm.

Girl's Denim Jean Jacket

INSTRUCTIONS:

1. Cut off jacket cuffs. Cut off a portion of the lower band just beneath the last snap or button.

2. Cut out insets beneath front pockets, between seams.

3. On right lower sleeve, cut out 2 vertical rectangles to hold images. Be sure to make the opening a little smaller than the image. Make one about 1" above the lower edge and another about 1 ½" above lower edge.

4. Machine wash and dry the garment to fray the raw edges.

5. **Collar** — With a seam ripper, remove the collar. Iron the collar flat and trace it onto paper. Draw another line ½" out from this line all around to add seam allowance. On the collar edge that was

IMAGES USED:

- **Carte Postale** 5" x 3 ½" on cotton poplin

- **Japan Text** 8" x 10" on cotton poplin

- **2 Water Lily images** 6" x 4" on canvas

- **Butterfly Pink Blooms** 4" x 6" on linen

- **2 Morpho Butterfly:** 4 ½" x 7" on linen and 2 ¼" x 3 ½" on cotton poplin

- **2 Tuck Birds:** 2 ½" x 3 ½" on iron–on transfer and about 2 ½" x 3 ½" on cotton poplin

- **Cashmiriana** 2 ¼" x 3 ½" on canvas

connected to the neck of the jacket, draw a notch. Cut out 2 collars using this pattern. *(See Diagram A.)*

Cut out and attach interface if necessary. Pin and stitch trim to the right side of one collar, aligning edges so that trim points inward. *(See Diagram B.)*

6. With RST*, pin and stitch collars together using a ½" seam, leaving the notched edge open. Trim corners, turn and press. Press under open notched edge ½". Slide the collar over the exposed jacket neck edge with

*RST = right sides together

Diagram A

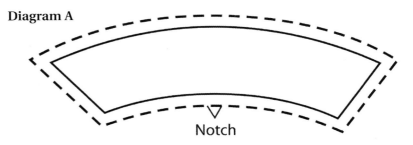

Notch

Dashed line indicates ½" seam allowance

Diagram B

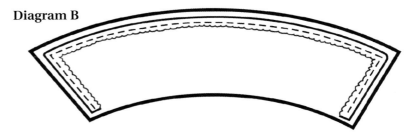

right side up and pin in place. Stitch close to the folded edge, being careful to catch collar beneath.

7. **Sleeves** – From canvas, cut out the Cashmiriana image to fit the smaller opening. Cut it a bit larger than that opening so you can stitch it in place. Pin the image beneath the opening and zigzag around the edges with a contrasting thread. From poplin, cut out the small Morpho Butterfly to fit the larger opening (leaving an extra border). Pin it in place beneath the opening and stitch, using a straight stitch with contrasting thread (green). With 3 strands of embroidery floss (pink), add a running stitch outside this first machine stitching.

8. Following the manufacturer's directions, insert eyelets about 1 ½" apart around the lower edge of the sleeve.

9. Cut 2 triangles of fabric to serve as insets in the side seam of sleeve. *(See photo below)*. Serge all edges of these insets if possible. Use a seam ripper to remove some of the side seam above the inset if desired. Place the inset under the opening and pin in place. Use your machine to zigzag up each side as far as possible (green used). Use 3 strands embroidery floss (blue) to add a running stitch to attach the remaining inset. *(See stitch diagram on page 127.)*

10. **Front Insets** – Measure the opening height. Using your favorite fabric scraps, piece together a length to fit these openings. Be certain to make them wide enough to extend beyond the opening edges. Place a scrap of lace on top if you wish. Use the cropped Tuck Bird image as a section if desired. Serge the outer edges of the completed inset fabric if possible. Pin in place beneath the opening. Machine-stitch with denim colored thread to attach along the jacket seams.

11. **Jacket Front** – Trace upper left or right front top piece above the horizontal seam. Cut out this shape and use it as a pattern to cut out the Water Lily images. Be sure to make 2 opposite pieces (reverse one). It does not need to fit pattern exactly. Apply Lite Seam-a-Seam® to the image backs according to manufacturer's directions and iron in place. Using a contrasting thread (orange used), attach with a wide zigzag stitch down each side and across the bottom of the image.

12. **Circular Front Button Embellishments** (right or left front; whichever is on top when your jacket is closed)– **Middle button:** cut a circle of wool about 1 ¾" in diameter with pinking sheers. Cut a slightly smaller sheer fabric circle with pinking sheers. Center on wool circle. Position circles between snaps or buttons and sew a button through center through all thicknesses. **Top and bottom buttons:** cut 2 more circles of wool with pinking sheers. Cut 2 smaller circles of wool in a different color.

Center on first circles. Place these between snaps or buttons and sew in place with a button in the center.

13. **Jacket Back** – Fold the fabric with the Japan Text image in half vertically. On the wrong side, draw a curving line beginning at fold and expanding out to 3" at lower edge. *(See photo of jacket's back on page 29 for example.)* Cut along the curved line and down the center. Apply Lite Steam-a-Seam® to the back of each piece. Position along vertical seams of back. Iron on. With contrasting thread (rose), zigzag around curved and lower edge.

14. **Center Collage** – Cut a scrap of your favorite fabric 3 ½" x 3 ¼". Serge the edges. Cut out the red-breasted bird image from iron-on fabric. Iron it to the center of this fabric. This will be one element of your collage.

15. Arrange these images—Carte Postale, Butterfly Pink Blooms, MorphoButterfly—and the Tuck Bird square as shown in photograph. You may apply these with Lite Steam-a-Seam® or turn them under ¼", press, and stitch in place. Use contrasting thread around one or more elements for interest.

16. **Lower Edge** – Open out the jacket and measure the lower edge. Cut a length of pom poms to fit plus 1" extra. Slip this under the frayed band so only the pom poms are exposed. Hand-sew to band using strong thread in a running stitch. Turn the ends under ½" and tack them to the jacket.

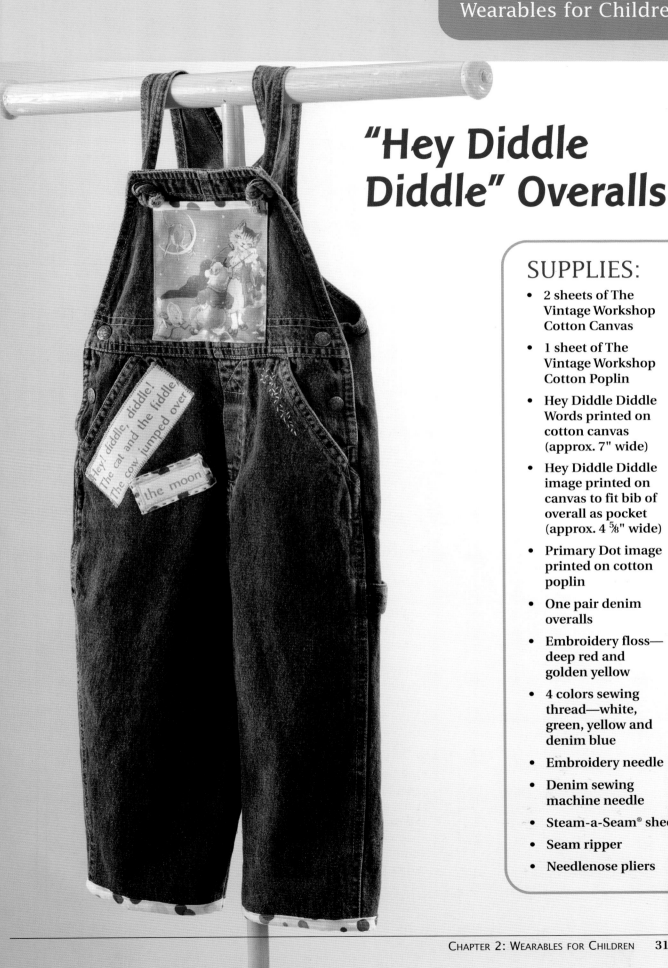

"Hey Diddle Diddle" Overalls

SUPPLIES:

- 2 sheets of The Vintage Workshop Cotton Canvas

- 1 sheet of The Vintage Workshop Cotton Poplin

- Hey Diddle Diddle Words printed on cotton canvas (approx. 7" wide)

- Hey Diddle Diddle image printed on canvas to fit bib of overall as pocket (approx. 4 ⅝" wide)

- Primary Dot image printed on cotton poplin

- One pair denim overalls

- Embroidery floss— deep red and golden yellow

- 4 colors sewing thread—white, green, yellow and denim blue

- Embroidery needle

- Denim sewing machine needle

- Steam-a-Seam® sheet

- Seam ripper

- Needlenose pliers

INSTRUCTIONS:

Turn a plain pair of denim overalls into a keepsake. This timeless, playfully embellished garment is suitable for boys or girls and makes a unique gift for anyone. A vibrantly colored vintage illustration of "Hey Diddle Diddle" makes a cheerful statement on the bib as a pocket. It is subtly trimmed with a vintage dot fabric that you can print from the CD along with the image. The verse itself is enlarged and appliquéd to the overalls, lending a great graphic element. With a touch of fabric encircling the hem and a few stitches of embroidery, your child is good to go in a fun, yet functional garment.

1. Cut off hems of overall legs.

2. With pliers, remove metal buttons from overall bib.

3. Remove clips from overall straps.

4. Where the buttons were removed, stitch a buttonhole large enough to pull the straps through.

5. Cut out the pocket-sized Hey Diddle Diddle image from fabric to fit your overalls. Be sure to allow an extra ½" on the sides and lower edge to turn under.

6. Measure the top width of your image (including hems) and cut a strip of Primary Dot fabric this width x 1 ¼". Fold in half lengthwise and press. Turn under long edges ¼" and press. Place this over top of pocket with raw edge resting in crease of binding. Stitch across, near lower fold of binding.

7. If you have a serger, serge sides and lower edge of pocket. Press under ½" along sides and lower edge. Pin to center of bib. Stitch close to turned under edges.

8. From the Hey Diddle Diddle words only image, cut out the verse as shown:

   Hey! Diddle, diddle!
   The cat and the fiddle,
   The cow jumped over

Cut out "the moon" separately, leaving as much white space as possible around the words. "The moon" should measure approximately 2 ½" x ⅞".

9. Following manufacturer's directions, apply Steam-a-Seam® to the back of large verse image and place it diagonally along the right pocket. Iron it in place. Using green thread, zigzag around the outer border. You will need to unsnap the overalls and stitch through the pocket beneath.

10. From the Primary Dot fabric, cut a 3 ½" x 1 ¾" rectangle. Press the edges under ¼". Place at an angle with the upper right corner overlapping the large verse slightly. Pin. With red embroidery floss, add a running stitch through all thicknesses around the perimeter to secure.

11. Apply Steam-a-Seam® to the back of "the moon". Iron it onto the center of the rectangle. Using yellow thread, machine stitch around the verse with an appliqué or small zigzag stitch.

12. On the left pocket, use 3 to 4 strands of deep red floss to stitch along pocket opening in the pattern shown. Use golden yellow embroidery floss to add a random seed stitch on the upper pocket, and trailing down. *(See Stitch Diagram page 127.)*

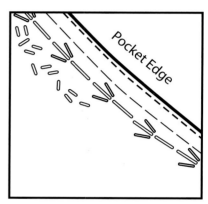

13. Use a seam ripper to remove 8" or 9" of inner leg seams beginning at the lower leg. Measure the width of the lower leg when the seam is removed. From the Primary Dot fabric, cut a strip for each leg that is this width x 1 ½". Fold the strip in half lengthwise and press. Turn under the long edges ¼" and press. Place this "binding" over the lower leg with the raw edge resting in the crease. Stitch close to the folded edge.

14. Turn overalls inside out and with RST*, restitch the pant legs along the original seam line. Serge the seam allowance if desired.

15. Pull the overall straps through the buttonholes and knot to secure.

*RST=right sides together

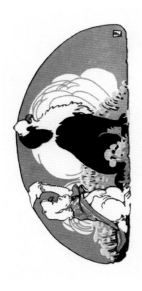

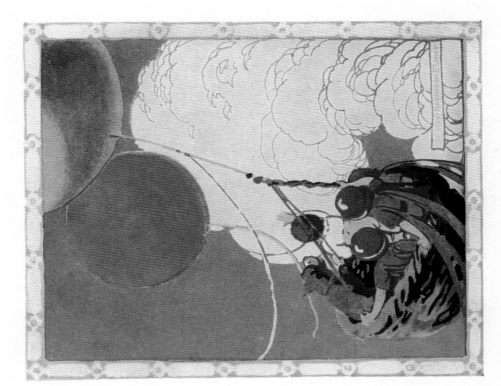

abcdefghijklmnopqrstuvwxyz

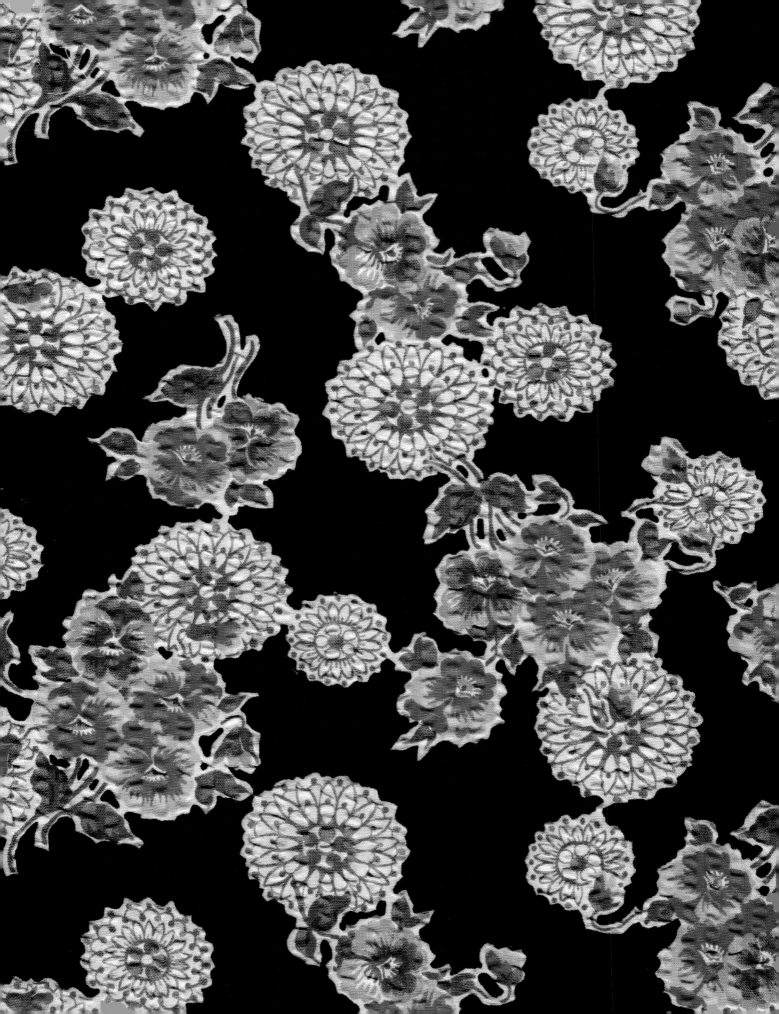

Nymphæa Caspary

心として面積56,923陷が指定され、次いで昭

原、鬼怒川、川治、庚申山等が編入され総面

なりました。その中心地日光は東京より3時

の名はあまりにも世間に有名であります。こ

の粋をつくして建造された輪王寺を始めとし

院等のけんらん豪華なる人工美と、そして又

碧の水をた丶えた中禅寺湖、通称「日光48滝

広大なる戦場ヶ原等、春は新緑、秋は紅葉の

して結構という勿れ」の諺の通りであります

史、地理、理科等の生きた社会科の資料とし

の地であります。尾瀬ヶ原を中心として面積5

ら見学の案内書として、多方面より写真を掲

する次第であります。広大なる戦場ヶ原等、春

の開山にして、国立公園日光は昭和9年12月

心として面積56,923陷が指定され、次いで昭

原、鬼怒川、川治、庚申山等が編入され総面

なりました。その中心地日光は東京より3時

PLATE XXIX.

Morpho achilles

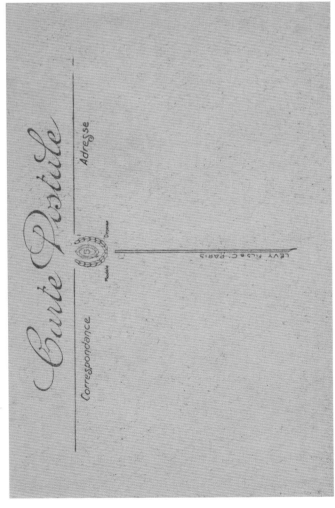

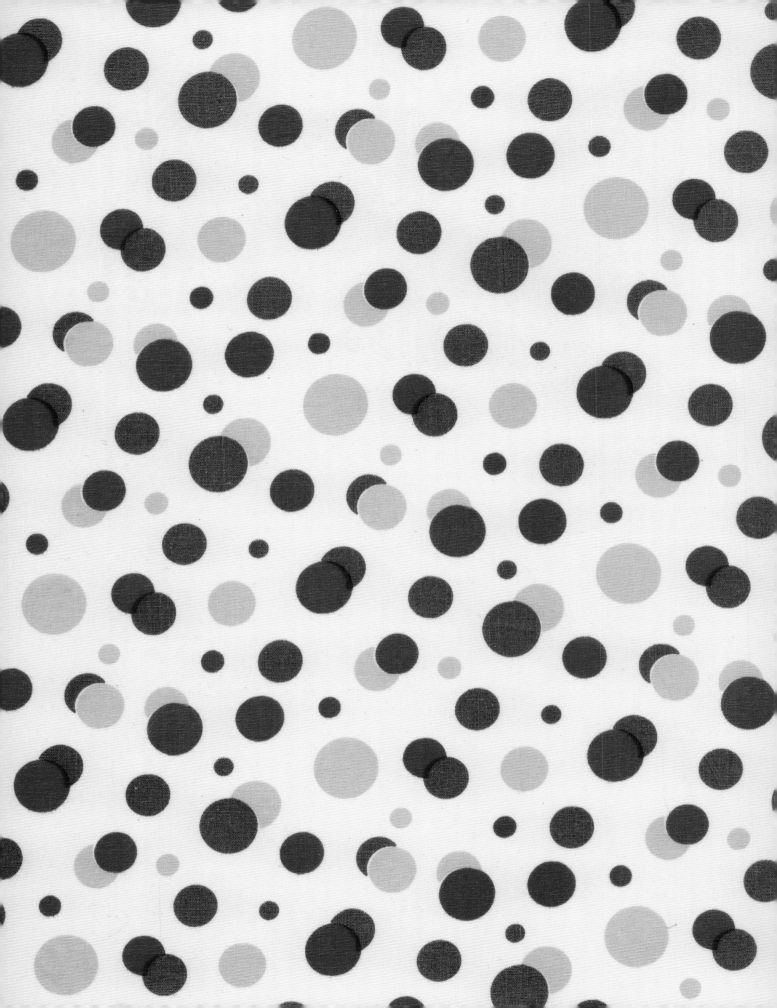

Hey! diddle, diddle!
The cat and the fiddle,
The cow jumped over the moon;

You Go Girls!

Retro

Welcome to the popular and ever-changing

world of Retro artwork! This chapter is chock-full of great art images that had their renaissance in the world of advertising. Designer t-shirts are being sold in record numbers and people are paying big dollars to buy artist-inspired retro fashion. Greeting card artists have been especially successful using retro images in the marketplace and now their popularity has seeped over into fashion. In this chapter, the designers at The Vintage Workshop present projects that have been inspired by this more recent era of art.

Retro art's graphic style developed for a reason. In the 30s, 40s, 50s, and 60s, the cost of creating detailed four-color separations and printing for mass audiences was prohibitive. Ad agencies turned their attention to developing clean art with very graphic boundaries that could be developed and printed economically. That is why so much of the art that has become popular comes from advertising posters and magazine ads. Collections of black-and-white photography have also come into vogue. Check The Vintage Workshop frequently for our expanding collection of retro offerings.

With a little creativity you can create your own unique look for a fraction of the designer prices. We hope you enjoy our interpretations of this retro craze.

Asian Denim Jacket

The mystery of the Far East is the muse behind this denim jacket that blurs the line between elegant and eclectic. It is at once opulent and graced with effortless ease. The back is gorgeously adorned with a litany of rich hues and textures with just a smattering of crystals for shine. A velvet collar replaces the denim and one front pocket is dramatically transformed with a brocade overlay. An interplay of images and stitches is seen at the shoulder and descending to one inset on the front.

SUPPLIES:

- **2 sheets The Vintage Workshop Iron-on Transfer II**
- **3 sheets The Vintage Workshop Cotton Poplin**
- **1 sheet The Vintage Workshop Linen**
- **1 sheet The Vintage Workshop Silk**
- **One denim jacket preferably with buttons instead of snaps. Sample jacket is a non-traditional style with a shirttail hem.**
- **Fabric for collar (velvet used for sample)**
- **2 vintage or new ⅞ – 1" buttons for front pockets**
- **Needlenose pliers (to remove jacket buttons)**
- **Small piece of fabric for pocket**
- **Shortcut to Style™ embellishing tool (optional) with clear, peridot and topaz crystals**
- **4 fabrics to blend with Asian theme**
- **Lite Steam-a-Seam® sheet**
- **Paper to make pattern, preferably tracing or vellum**
- **Seam ripper**
- **Thread in assorted colors for decorative stitching and image appliqué**
- **Denim sewing machine needle**

INSTRUCTIONS:

1. **Collar** – With seam ripper, remove collar. Iron flat. Trace onto paper. Enlarge this by ½" all around to add seam allowance. *(See illustration below.)* On the edge that connects to the jacket neck, draw a notch. Cut out this pattern and use it to cut 2 collars from fabric, adding interfacing if necessary. With RST*, pin and stitch collars together with a ½" seam, leaving the notched edge open. Trim corners, turn and press.

2. **Jacket Front** – Print the Chinese Postmark image on 8" x 10" cotton poplin. On paper, trace the jacket's upper left front above the horizontal seam. Cut out this shape and use it as a pattern to cut out the Chinese Postmark. Apply Lite Steam-a-Seam® to the image back and iron it onto the jacket. Add a decorative stitch to the lower and inner edge of the image. If desired, stitch random curves diagonally across the image.

3. **Pockets** – If your jacket has patch pockets, remove the right front pocket with a seam ripper and trace the pocket to make a pattern. If the pocket cannot be removed, trace the shape and cut that out for the pattern. From fabric, cut out one pocket—**adding** ¼" to sides and lower edge and 1" to the top edge. Serge the edges if desired. Press the top edge under 1", then stitch across ¾" from top. Press the sides and lower edge under ¼". Pin the pocket in place and stitch close to the sides and lower edge. Fold the demin pocket flap down and sew on a button.

*RST = right sides together

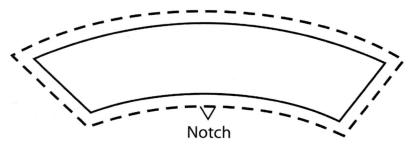

Notch

Dashed line indicates ½" seam allowance

IMAGES USED:

- Temple Collage
- Beautiful Geisha
- Chinatown Night
- Weighing Baby
- Chinese Postmark
- Chinese Postcard
- Japanese Lanterns
- Geisha Laundry
- Japanese Field

4. **Front Inset and Sleeve** – The right front inset contains 3 images. The top and bottom images (Chinese Postmark and Chinese Postcard) are printed on an iron-on sheet. Trim these to fit the available space and iron them to the inset, inside the seams. The center image is Japanese Field, printed on cotton poplin. Cut this from fabric, allowing extra around the edges to turn under. Stitch it in place inside the inset, slightly overlapping the images already in place above and below it. Apply decorative stitching around the edge of the image, if desired. Now turn the jacket wrong side out. On the end of one sleeve or cuff, apply iron-on images. Our sample uses portions of the Geisha Laundry and Chinese Postcard images. When you roll up your sleeve or cuff, the images will be visible.

5. **Back Collage** – Print the following images: Temple Collage on 8" x 10" linen, Chinatown Night on a 10" length of silk, Weighing Baby on 5" x 7" cotton poplin, Beautiful Geisha on $3\frac{1}{2}$" x 5" cotton poplin, Japanese Lanterns on $2\frac{1}{2}$" x $5\frac{1}{2}$" cotton poplin, and Chinese Postmark and Chinese Postcard on a $3\frac{1}{2}$" square iron-on sheet. Make a paper pattern of the upper third and lower third of the jacket's middle inset. Using this pattern as a guide, piece together 3 fabrics to fill the lower third of the inset. Apply decorative stitching across the connecting seams. Add a running stitch with quilting thread across one section if desired. Turn under the edges, press and stitch in place inside the jacket seams. Again using the pattern as a guide, cut a piece of fabric to cover the upper third of the inset. Allow extra at the edges to turn under. Press under this allowance and stitch the fabric to the upper portion of the inset, inside the seams.

- Our directions will guide you to make the collage as shown but feel free to alter it as you wish. Begin with the upper back yoke of the jacket. To the left and right of center, iron on the Chinese Postcard and Postmark images. Tilt them slightly out.

- Cut out the Beautiful Geisha image from fabric, adding $\frac{1}{4}$" on all sides. Press under the edges and pin the image at an angle in the center. Stitch the edges with a narrow zigzag stitch in a contrasting color.

- Cut out the Temple Collage from fabric, adding $\frac{1}{4}$" on all sides. Press under the edges and pin to the center back at an angle. *(See large photo of back at left)*. Stitch in place.

- Cut out Weighing Baby from fabric, adding $\frac{1}{4}$" on all sides. Press under the edges and pin it in place diagonally overlapping the lower right corner of the Temple Collage. Stitch close to edges.

- Cut Chinatown Night from fabric, adding $\frac{1}{4}$" on all sides. Press under the edges and pin it to the left of the Temple Collage, overlapping the lower corner. Zigzag or appliqué around the edges with contrasting thread.

- Across the top of the Chinatown image, stitch the Japanese Lanterns to add a horizontal element.

- If desired, use the Shortcut to Style™ tool to add crystals to the center image. Our jacket has a row of clear crystals along the bottom, topaz crystals on the top flower, and 5 peridot crystals in a vertical line on the green image edge.

Kitschy Kitchen Apron

Many advertising images featured women in the kitchen demonstrating new appliances, like the classic image shown on this apron. The humor of an oven full of delightful home cooked food, coupled with the command to "come and get it," captures the essence of the Retro movement. The hair and dress are definitely "June Cleaver" style. Today this image is truly retro— with the dawn of fast food and modern appliances.

INSTRUCTIONS:

1. From the CD, print the Suzy Homemaker image and "Come and Get It" text, following the manufacturer's instructions.

2. Using scissors or a craft knife, cut out the images exactly around the edges.

3. Carefully remove the paper backing from the images and center the Suzy Homemaker image 1½" from top edge of the apron. Iron it in place following the manufacturer's instructions.

4. Place "Come and Get It" centered, partially on top of kitchen image *(see project photo for reference)*, and iron into place.

SUPPLIES:

- 2 sheets The Vintage Workshop Iron-on Transfer II
- Suzy Homemaker image (printed size approx. 7 ¼" x 6")
- Come and Get It text image (printed size approx. 6 ¾" wide)
- 1 canvas apron (manufactured by Bagworks™) pre-washed
- Scissors or craft knife and cutting mat

Women's Work Apron

INSTRUCTIONS:

1. From the CD, print the Woman's Job image and 2 retro prints (approximately 5"x 5") to the iron-on transfer sheets, following the manufacturer's instructions.

2. Using scissors or a craft knife, cut the images out exactly around the edges.

3. Carefully remove the paper backing from the images and center the Woman's Job image on the center pocket of the tool belt. Iron it into place following the manufacturer's instructions.

4. Before ironing the retro prints in place to the outside pockets, trim them to fit inside the pocket.

5. Align the retro pocket images squarely in place and iron, following the manufacturer's instructions.

SUPPLIES:

- **2 sheets The Vintage Workshop Iron-on Transfer II**

- **Woman's Job image (printed size is approx. 4" x 5 ½")**

- **Teal and Zigzag Scrap images (printed size is approx. 5" x 5")**

- **1 canvas 3-pocket tool belt (manufactured by Bagworks), pre-washed**

- **Scissors or craft knife and cutting mat**

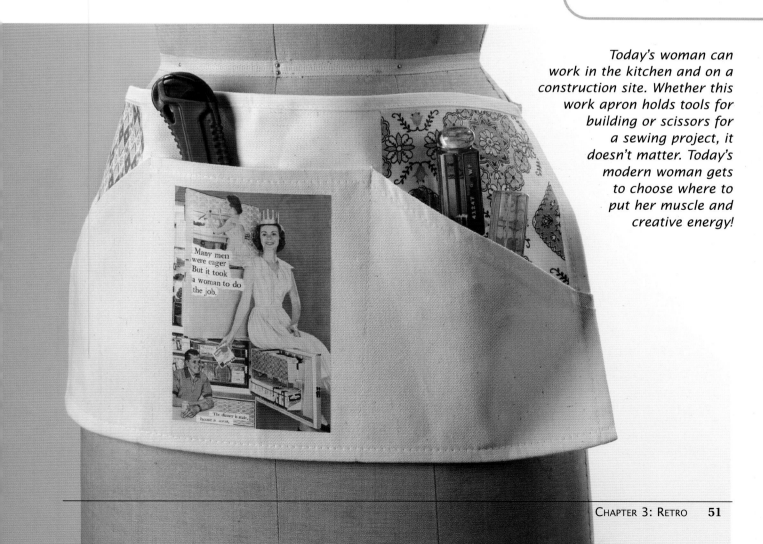

Today's woman can work in the kitchen and on a construction site. Whether this work apron holds tools for building or scissors for a sewing project, it doesn't matter. Today's modern woman gets to choose where to put her muscle and creative energy!

Classic Fashion Clutch

The beauty in this little hard-shell clutch is in the eye of the beholder, but is also so easy to make that you'll find yourself customizing all of your outfits. It's easy to revise this fashion statement over and over again if you use the optional Adhesive-backed fabric that is noted as optional in the supply list. It allows you to simply peel away the images and choose a new one to match your latest outfit.

SUPPLIES:

- **2 sheets (for front and back) The Vintage Workshop Cotton Poplin**
- **Shoe Quote image (printed size is approx. 8 ½" x 5 ½")**
- **Classic Clutch hard shell plastic purse**
- **June Tailor Fray Block® to seal cut edges of fabric**
- **Craft glue—we recommend Gem-Tac or Fabric–Tac from Beacon**
- **Popsicle or craft stick for applying glue**
- **Sandpaper**
- **Craft knife and mat**

OPTIONAL:

- **Use The Vintage Workshop adhesive-backed fabric and simply trim, peel back paper and adhere to clutch**

INSTRUCTIONS:

1. Print Shoe Quote image (8½" x 5½") onto inkjet fabric sheets.

2. If using cotton poplin, remove the paper backing and saturate all edges of the images with FrayBlock. Allow to dry and then cut out the images exactly around all edges

3. Use the sandpaper to "rough up" the sides of the clutch. You want to remove as much of the sheen as possible so the glue will adhere properly. Wipe off the clutch with a damp cloth to remove any small particles.

4. Beginning on one side, apply glue to the clutch and smooth it out with your fingers or a Popsicle stick.

5. Press the image into place, making sure the fabric is smooth. Wipe away any excess glue. If you use cotton poplin, apply FrayBlock again around all edges.

6. Repeat the process on the other side of the clutch.

Timeless Travels Handbag

INSTRUCTIONS:

1. Print any of the larger images from the CD or use purchased papers to fit templates for the handbag.

   Approximate sizes are:
   - front $7\frac{5}{8}$" x $5\frac{3}{4}$"
   - back $5\frac{1}{8}$" x $7\frac{3}{4}$"
   - sides $4\frac{1}{2}$" x $5\frac{3}{4}$"

2. Trim images to fit each side of the bag and insert, following manufacturer's instructions.

SUPPLIES:

- **Creative Clazzic Handbag by Z Becky Brown**
- **Large images from CD printed on inkjet printable paper or use The Vintage Workshop's Travel scrapbook papers: Currency, Western Hemisphere, and Postal Words** *(available from Paper Adventures by ANW/Crestwood, see Resources on page 127)*
- **Craft knife and cutting mat**

This purse features Vintage Workshop artwork cut and placed as inserts between the clear plastic of the bag and a stiff interior liner that holds and protects the paper designs. You may choose to print images from the CD or use purchased scrapbook papers to create this smart bag. Prepare several Vintage Workshop designs as inserts that can be easily changed out to go with what you're wearing.

Rodeo Jacket

SUPPLIES:

- 2 sheets The Vintage Workshop Cotton Poplin
- 1 sheet The Vintage Workshop Linen
- 1 sheet The Vintage Workshop Canvas
- One light colored denim jacket
- Thread in assorted colors for decorative stitching
- White thread
- 7 mismatched ⅝" – ¾" buttons, vintage or new
- Needlenose pliers
- Pinking sheers
- 2 zippers, 9" or longer, preferably with metal teeth. Vintage zippers look great, but upholstery zippers trimmed to fit are another good option.
- Fabric for collar
- Assorted vintage feedsack prints printed on cotton or purchased fabrics
- Seam ripper
- Fabric strips to border cowboy couple image on jacket back
- Lite Steam-a-Seam® sheet
- Paper for patterns, preferably tissue or vellum
- Embroidery floss and needle

Whoa! Here's a wheat-colored denim jacket all spruced up to take you on a western jaunt. Hand-colored vintage postcards lend inspiration to this distinctive creation. The back image is framed with well-used vintage zippers, hand-stitched over nostalgic feed sack borders. The front pockets, crowned with vintage rhinestone buttons, are created with raw-edged snippets of vintage feed sacks and text. Within the front insets, go to town with your machine's decorative stitches that you might not have had the occasion to try. A new collar emerges, awash with the soft hues of an antique blanket.

IMAGES USED:

- *The Trail of the Lonesome Pine* sheet music image printed on 8" x 10" cotton poplin
- Rodeo Program image (approx. 4 ¾" x 1 ¾") printed on cotton poplin
- Rodeo Rope image (approx. 2 ½" x 1 ¾") printed on cotton poplin
- Blue Cowboy image (approx. 3 ¼" x 3 ¾") printed on cotton poplin
- Cowboy Couple printed on 8" x 10" canvas
- Linen Cowboy printed on 3 ½" x 5" linen

INSTRUCTIONS:

1. **Collar** – Remove collar with a seam ripper. Iron flat. Trace onto paper. Enlarge by ½" to add seam allowance. On the edge that was connected to the jacket neck, draw a notch. *(See diagram on top of page 56.)* Cut out the pattern and use it to cut 2 collars from fabric. Interface if necessary.

2. With RST*, stitch collars together with a ½" seam, leaving the notched edge open. Trim corners, turn and press. Press the notched edge under ½". Slide it over the exposed jacket neck edge with right side up and pin in place. Stitch close to the top folded edge, being careful to catch the folded edge beneath.

3. **Buttons** – With needlenose pliers, remove the buttons down the jacket front and front pockets if applicable. Replace those buttons with your mismatched buttons.

*RST = Right Sides Together

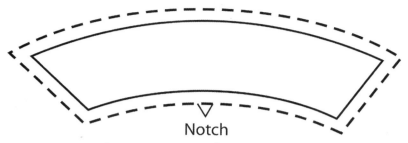

Notch

Dashed line indicates ½" seam allowance

4. **Pockets** – If the front pockets are patch pockets, remove them with a seam ripper and trace them to make a pattern. Add ¼" all around to turn under. If the front pockets cannot be removed, trace around their shape on paper and add ¼" all around. Cut out the pattern.

5. Use a lightweight cotton as an underpocket. Cut 2 underpockets from your pattern. Press under ¼" on all sides and stitch close to the fold.

6. Now, cut strips of vintage feed sacks or cottons (use pinking shears for some), to layer one over another to cover this underpocket. You may also use text from the Rodeo Program printed cotton poplin. Leave the edges raw. Secure some of the strips with decorative stitching.

7. Trim the pocket bottom and top edge flush with the underpocket. Leave the edges raw. Turn the sides under ¼" and stitch to the under pocket. Pin the pocket under the flap in original position and stitch in place.

8. Sew buttons on pockets beneath buttonholes in flaps.

9. **Front collage** – Trace the upper left front jacket section above the horizontal seam. Cut out this pattern and use it to cut out a section of the sheet music. See sample. (Save the sheet music title intact for use in another area.)

10. Apply Lite Steam-a-Seam® to the image back and iron to upper left jacket section.

11. From the cotton poplin, cut out the word "Rodeo," adding a ⅜" border. Cut out the Blue Cowboy plus a ¼" border. From the sheet music, cut out the title and the first line of music beneath it.

Turn the Blue Cowboy edges under ¼" and press. Pin in place diagonally to upper right jacket front and zigzag around edge.

12. Next, make a horizontal pleat in the sheet music piece. Turn under the edges. Press and pin in place diagonally to upper right jacket front, overlapping the cowboy image. Zigzag

around the edges. With embroidery floss, add a running stitch through the pleat.

13. Turn under ¼" around the Rodeo Rope image and press. Pin it to upper right also, overlapping the sheet music. Use a blanket stitch around the edges to secure.

14. **Back of Jacket** – Crop the Cowboy Couple photo as desired. With pinking sheers, cut 2 strips of 1" wide fabric that is 2" longer than the image sides. Cut 2 more that are 2" longer than top and bottom edge of the image.

15. Center the image on the jacket back. Place the fabric strips just under the edges. Stitch in place close to the image edge.

16. Open up the zippers. Place one pull at the top left corner and one at bottom right. Trim zippers to fit. With needle and white thread, add a running stitch through the zipper tape to secure it.

17. With pinking sheers, cut around Linen Cowboy image, leaving a white border. Pin the image at a diagonal over the lower left corner of large image and stitch close to edges. Trim the zipper so that it ends just under right side of the cowboy.

Retro T-shirts

Why pay an arm and a leg for designer t-shirts when you can customize your own using some of our great collected images? The ones that our designers have put together on these pages use a variety of t-shirt styles because there are so many to choose from today. Making your own embellished t-shirts is probably the easiest project possible with Iron-on transfers or printable fabrics. There are some basic instructions to follow, as directed by the manufacturer. The Vintage Workshop designers use our own Iron-on Transfer I or Iron-on Transfer II in these projects. Iron-on Transfer I is translucent. allowing some show-through of color from the garment. Iron-on II may also be used, but it will be opaque.

SUPPLIES:

- **Beading thread**
- **Beading/sewing needles**
- **Rotary cutter/ scissors**
- **Ruler**

FAIRY PRINCESS T

- **1 sheet The Vintage Workshop Cotton Poplin**
- **Butterfly Girl image (from Chapter 3) printed on cotton poplin**
- **Fairy Princess sentiment (approx. 4 ¾" wide) printed on cotton poplin**
- **One long sleeved plum t-shirt**
- **One package ½" gold star sequins**
- **One package metallic gold seed beads**
- **One package copper seed beads**
- **One package tiny lavender Swarovski® crystals**
- **DMC embroidery floss #E3821 metallic gold and #317 dark gray**
- **Dark gray and light pink sewing thread**

YOU GO GIRLS! T

- **2 sheets The Vintage Workshop Cotton Poplin**
- **Dotty Floral image (approx. 6" square) printed on cotton poplin**
- **One Water Ballet image (approx. 6" x 3 ⅞") printed on cotton poplin**
- **"You Go Girls!" sentiment printed on cotton poplin (approx. 3" wide)**
- **One short-sleeved light blue tissue t-shirt with taupe trim**
- **One package 5mm clear and one package 4mm pink iridescent sequins**
- **One package silver bugle beads, ¼" long**
- **One package each clear and pink seed beads**
- **DMC ecru embroidery floss**
- **Light blue and white sewing thread**

Fairy Princess T-shirt

INSTRUCTIONS:

1. Cut out the image and sentiment from cotton poplin, leaving ¼" white border around Butterfly Girl and ½" border around "Fairy Princess" words. Remove paper backings. Turn under ¼" edges on fairy image and press. Turn under edges on sentiment so it has a ³⁄₁₆" border all around the words. Press. Center the Butterfly Girl image on front of shirt as desired. Pin and baste in place. Center the "Fairy Princess" sentiment beneath fairy image. Pin and baste. With gray thread, hand-stitch the fairy image to the shirt using tiny stitches around the outer edges. Repeat this with pink thread for the sentiment. Remove the basting and quilt around the fairy wings and dress with dark gray thread, using a running stitch.

2. With beading thread, hand-stitch the copper seed beads around the outer edges of the images, spacing the beads ¼" apart. *(See the stitch diagram on page 127 for technique.)*

3. With 2 strands metallic gold floss and using a back stitch, make a diagonal wand from fairy's hand over her shoulder on the left side. Extend the wand into the background ¾". Sew a star sequin/gold seed bead to the end of the wand with beading thread. *(See the diagram on page 127 for technique.)*

4. Randomly stitch lavender crystals to wings with beading thread.

5. Finish the shirt by adding a blanket stitch at the neckline and around the armholes using 3 strands of dark gray floss.

You Go Girls! T-shirt

INSTRUCTIONS:

1. Cut out the Water Ballet image and Dotty Floral image, leaving a ¼" white border all around. Cut out the sentiment with a ½" border all around. Press under ¼" borders on girls and floral print. Press under the borders on the sentiment so there is ⅛" all around.

2. Mark the shirt center front by measuring in from the side seams—mark the center with a basting thread. Position the floral square on the shirt front so it is off-center by 4" on the right side and 1 ¾" on left side. The upper edge of the square should be about 3" below the upper neck edge. Pin in place. With 2 strands ecru floss, secure the square to the shirt with a running stitch ⅛" from outer edges all around.

3. Position the Water Ballet image so it is centered on the shirt, 1" below upper edge of floral square. The girls image will jut out to the left of the floral print by 1 ¼". Pin. Place the sentiment below the girl image with

left side and upper edge flush with girl image. Pin. Hand-stitch the skiing girls and the sentiment in place around the outer edges, through all thicknesses.

4. Sew clear sequins/seed beads to the hems of the white dresses. Sew pink sequins/beads to the hem of pink dress.

5. Sew silver bugle beads in curved lines behind the skiers as shown in the photo. *(Refer to the diagram on page 127 for technique.)*

Travel Collage T-shirt

INSTRUCTIONS:

The Vintage Workshop Iron-on Transfer I is used in this project. It is translucent, allowing some color from the garment it is placed on to show through. Iron-on II may also be used, but it will be opaque.

1. From the CD, print the Travel Collage image.

2. Using scissors or a craft knife, cut out the images exactly around the edges.

3. Carefully remove the paper backing from the images and center the image 2" from the top edge of the shirt. Iron the image in place, following the manufacturer's instructions.

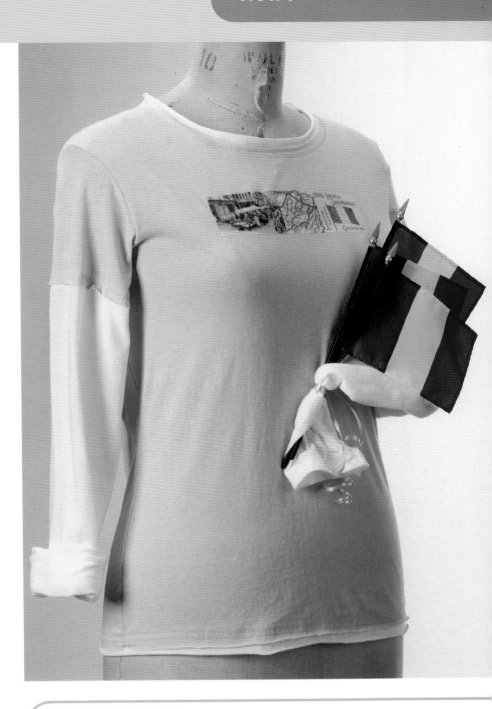

SUPPLIES:

- 1 sheet The Vintage Workshop Iron-on Transfer I
- Travel Collage image printed on transfer (printed size is approx. 7 ¼" wide)
- 1 t-shirt, pre-washed
- Scissors or craft knife and cutting mat

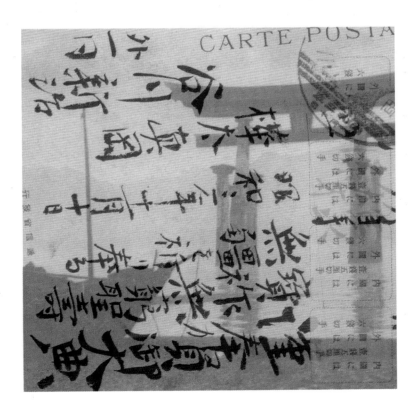

"Give a girl the right shoes and she can conquer the world."

—Bette Midler

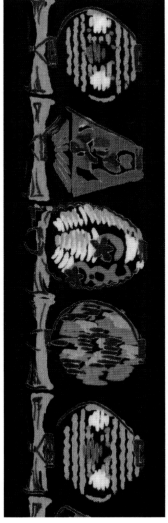

The Trail Of The Lonesome Pine

Words by
BALLARD MACDONALD

Music by
HARRY CARROLL

On a moun-tain
I can hear the

in Vir - gin - i - a stands a lone - some pine,_____
tink - ling wa - ter - fall, far a - mong the hills,_____

Just be - low is the cab - in home, Of a lit - tle
Blue - birds sing each so mer - ri - ly To his mate in

Come & GeT IT!

1944 Official Program Insert
LIST OF CONTESTANTS
GARDEN WORLD'S CHAMPIONSHIPS
The "Tophands" of the Western Range

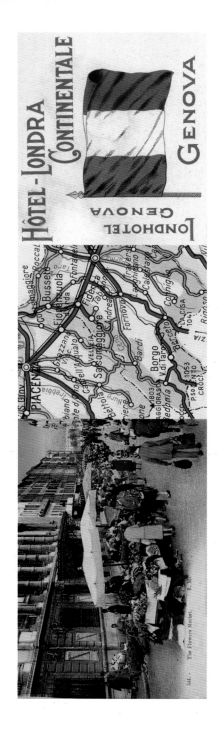

Many men were eager But it took a woman to do the job.

The dinner is stale, house a mess,

Note:

Fairy Princess
t-shirt uses
image from
Chapter 3,
page 35

Fairy Princess

Sophisticated Fashion

Welcome to our trunk show of trend-conscious, one-of-a-kind projects that are fresh, contemporary and truly for the adventurous seamstress. In vintage clothing and fashion accessories, it's true that what goes around, comes around. For those who seek the truly unusual and want to put their personal stamp on a signature style, we think the fashion statements found here will suit your desire to be independent and to step apart from the mass market crowd and be noticed.

The projects presented in this chapter are truly one-of-a-kind creations that will be treasured by their lucky owner. Our designers have looked at the current market and come up with their own personal statements of sophistication—with heavy emphasis on accessorizing with jewelry, belts, and embellished jeans.

Some of the techniques are a little more difficult than some of our earlier projects, but are so well worth the effort that goes into them. Soldered jewelry charms are big right now and we will teach you how to make your own using simple soldering techniques and some great images that we provide. If soldering is too complicated, you'll find an alternative to that here, too. The artwork and images that we have compiled to go along with these projects are sophisticated and versatile. Now you can make your own runway fashions—that are star quality!

Scarf

This fabulous scarf is truly a wearable work of art. Create an heirloom quality accessory using a montage of fabrics, embellishments, images and techniques. It is also a great way to use scraps of your beloved fabrics.

SUPPLIES:

- 1 sheet The Vintage Workshop Linen
- 1 sheet The Vintage Workshop Silk
- 1 sheet The Vintage Workshop Iron-On Transfer II
- 1 sheet The Vintage Workshop Cotton Poplin
- 1 sheet The Vintage Workshop Canvas
- Scarf lining fabric for 45" x 7"
- Assorted scraps of fabric such as velvet, vintage barkcloth, silk, recycled menswear wool, decorator fabric, brocade
- One package silk embroidery ribbon (green) and ribbon embroidery needle
- 4 buttons – any size (vintage rhinestone buttons used)
- 2 or 3 colors embroidery floss
- One scrap lace trim
- One piece lace, approximately 2 ½" x 3 ½"
- Pinking shears (optional)
- Assorted thread colors for decorative stitching
- Beads – Bead Soup used in Tomato Salsa color *(see Resources on page 127)*

INSTRUCTIONS:

Directions are provided using the fabrics in the sample, but of course, you may substitute any fabrics you choose. The scarf has five sections measuring 6 ¼" x 8", sewn together to create one length. Instructions are provided for each section: first for basic construction, then for embellishment.

All seams are ¼". **You will find all section illustrations on page 126.** In Illustration 1, note that Section 3 fits behind your neck, so no images are added there. Check that Sections 1, 2, 4 and 5 tops are all up—as others would see them around your neck. After you finish each section, trim it to 6 ¼" x 8". The approximate finished length is 39". Of course, if you want a longer scarf, feel free to add more sections.

Section 1 – Stitch French Lady RST*, along left side to a piece of vintage barkcloth. Place a narrower strip of barkcloth cut with pinking shears on top and attach it with a decorative stitch. Piece a scrap of silk and a piece of recycled menswear wool to make a 6 ¼" x 3" strip. With RST, stitch this to the first piece.

Section 2 – The lower half of Section 2 is a solid piece of vintage barkcloth. For the top half, left to right, piece together: silk, Nesting Birds image, and recycled wool. Add a square of Letters Montage. **Note:** Coffee was used to stain slightly the images of this section.

Section 3 – Piece together the fabrics as shown in the illustration.

Section 4 – The top half of this section is a solid piece of recycled menswear wool. Beneath this are pieced the Letter Montage and Ferris Wheel 2 images. Add a strip of velvet ¾" wide, cut with pinking shears and placed over the connecting seam. Connect it by stitching 7 irregular X's down the center with embroidery floss. From

an iron-on sheet, cut a section of the Russian PC Back that you find interesting. Iron it onto Letter Montage at a diagonal. With RST, stitch the top half to the bottom half.

Section 5 – The top third of this section is a decorator floral fabric. Use a floral if possible to embellish this as shown. The lower two-thirds of the section are comprised of the Queen Throne image on the left, then a strip of velvet above a square of wool. To the right of this is a strip of barkcloth cut with pinking shears. Add a strip of lace along the left edge of the velvet. With RST, stitch the Queen image to the pieced fabrics.

Embellishment Instructions:

Section 1 – Apply decorative stitching over the connecting seams with contrasting colored thread. Stitch 3 vintage rhinestone buttons horizontally on the wool. (You may want to add these after lining has been added to the scarf.)

*RST=right sides together

IMAGES USED:

- **French Lady** – 3 ¾" x 5 ¾" on silk
- **Queen Throne** – 3 ¼" x 6 ⅛" on silk
- **Coliseum** – 4" x 3 ½" on cotton poplin
- **Black Hat Lady** – 2 ¾" x 3 ¾" on cotton poplin
- **Ferris Wheel 2** – 2 ⅜" x 3 ¾" on linen
- **Russian PC Back** – one on linen and one on iron-on sheet (both 4 ½" x 3")
- **Nesting Birds** – 3" x 4 ¾" on cotton poplin
- **Letters Montage** – 8" x 10" on canvas
- **Travel Europe** – 4" x 4" on silk

Section 4 – From fabric, cut out the Travel image and position it on the upper wool piece at an angle. Attach it with an appliqué stitch. Cut out the Coliseum image and add a ¼" border. Press under this border and position the image to overlap the Travel Europe image at an angle. Add a blanket stitch around all the edges. Add a running stitch of silk embroidery ribbon all the way across, 1" from the top edge of this section.

Section 5 – Randomly sew small beads on the floral fabric. Sew larger beads radiating out from flower center. Apply a zigzag or decorator stitch vertically through barkcloth. Concentric circles were added to this velvet section also.

To Complete the Scarf:

Stitch together all the sections RST with a ¼" seam. Press. Use the completed scarf as a pattern for cutting out the lining to assure a perfect fit. Place the scarf and the lining RST and cut out the lining. Pin, then stitch, leaving a 5" opening to turn the right sides out. Turn, press and slipstitch the opening.

Section 2 – Cut out the Russian PC Back on linen with pinking shears, leaving a white border on all sides. Position the image diagonally, with the lower left corner overlapping Section 1. On top of this image (also overlapping the lower edge), place a rectangle of lace. Cut Black Hat Lady image from fabric the same size as the lace. Turn under a ¼" border on all sides, press and center this image on the lace. Stitch the edges with a zigzag stitch. Sew a vintage rhinestone button to the upper right corner of this image.

On the wool, add multiple diagonal running stitches with green silk embroidery ribbon. Cut out a small detail of the Russian PC Back image on an iron-on sheet. Iron this diagonally across the connecting seam of the bird and letter montage images.

Section 3 – Apply 4 different rows of decorator stitches horizontally across velvet 2. *(See Stitch Guide on page 127.)* On velvet 1, using embroidery floss, stitch concentric circles with a running stitch. *See Stitch Guide on page 127.*

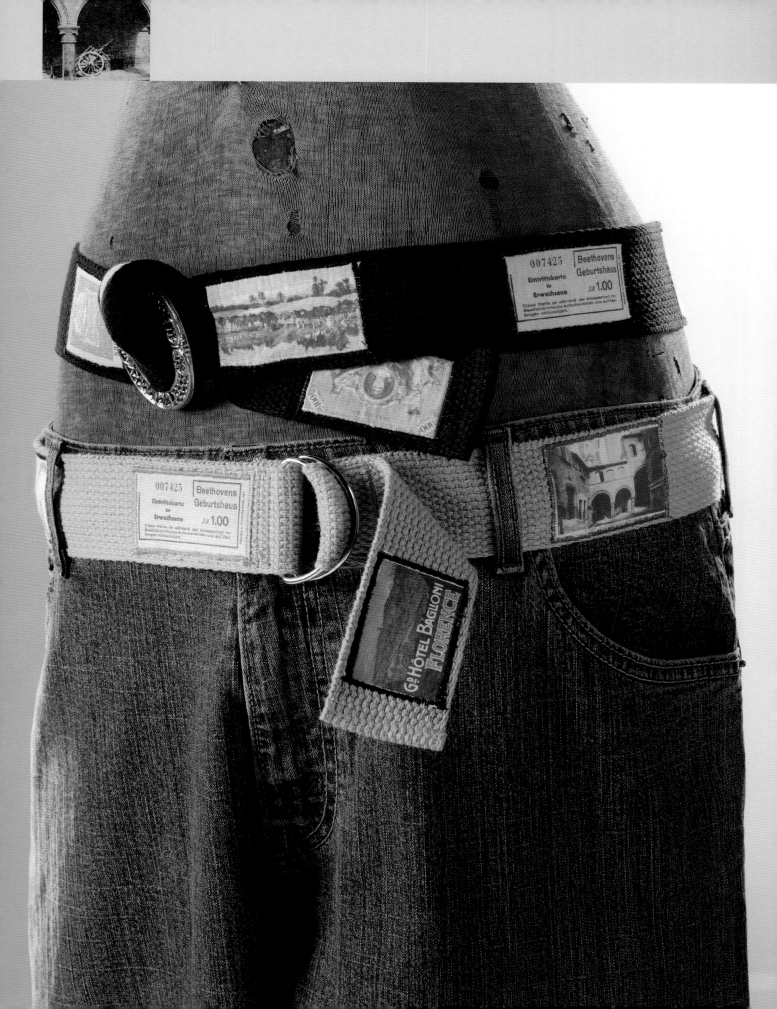

Belts

INSTRUCTIONS:

Celebrate your inner artist by encircling yourself with one of these unique belts. The fruit of your labor is a free-spirited travelogue of luggage tags, postcards from afar, foreign currency and a bit of whatnot. This easy project can be adapted to any images you fancy—and makes a smashing gift for a kindred spirit.

Black Belt

1. Make certain all images are applied in an upright position.

2. Apply Fray Check to both ends of the webbing and allow it to dry. Turn under one end ½" and stitch hem.

3. On the opposite end, apply the first image beginning 2" from end. Leave a space of about 2 ¼" to 2 ¾" between the images Spaces may vary slightly.

4. For all the images, follow these instructions: Print and cut images from fabric. No border is necessary. Following the manufacturer's directions, apply Steam-a-Seam® to each image back. Center the image and iron it onto the belt. The last image should be about 3/4" from the hemmed end.

5. After all the images are ironed on, adjust your sewing machine to an appliqué stitch. You may want to use a zigzag stitch set at a small stitch length. With black thread, stitch around every image, stitching over all fabric edges securely.

6. Pull the unhemmed end of the belt about 1" around the center bar of the buckle and stitch it in place.

Tan Belt

1. Follow Steps 1 through 3 of black belt but with 2 changes! Your last image should be applied to the wrong side of the belt because when belt is pulled through D-rings, the wrong side of the belt shows beyond the buckle. For this same reason, when you hem the end of your belt, turn it to what is at first the right side.

2. Follow Step 4 but instead of black thread, use a variety of colors if desired. The sample uses blue, black and tan.

3. Stack the D-rings and wrap the unhemmed end of the belt around both bars until about 1" is on the wrong side of the belt. Stitch across the end.

SUPPLIES:

- 1 sheet The Vintage Workshop cotton poplin

- 10 images* printed on cotton poplin. The image height should not exceed 1 ¾: Printed images may be of slightly different sizes.

- 2" wide black or tan belt webbing. To determine the length required, wrap a measuring tape around you at the point you will wear the belt. Add 7 ½" to this measurement.

- Steam-a-Seam® sheet

- 2" belt buckle. The black belt uses a buckle with a center bar. The tan belt uses D-rings (need 2).

- Thread to match webbing

- Contrasting thread if desired for appliqué. The tan belt uses blue, black and tan thread.

- Dritz Fray Check™

* The belts shown use 10 images. You may vary the number of images you use according to the length of your belt.

Embellished Jeans

You won't see yourself coming or going if you don these show-stopping jeans. You will be the conversation piece in jeans sporting pockets gleaming with beading and rich flecks of embroidery. A collage of images and ephemera in nostalgic hues ascend one leg. The back pockets are deconstructed and embellished with an antique palette of images, fabric, and stitching. Iridescent fabric paints orchestrate the finishing notes of this creation.

SUPPLIES:

- 5 sheets The Vintage Workshop Cotton Poplin
- One pair denim jeans
- Assortment of embroidery floss
- Embroidery needle
- Denim needle for sewing machine
- Seam ripper
- Pinking shears (not essential)
- Lite Steam-a-Seam®
- Beading needle (not too fragile)
- Assorted small beads: 2 packages Bead Soup used for sample— Tomato Salsa and Vichyssoise. A few other beads added as well for color variation.
- Artist's Paintstik by Shiva in iridescent color palette
- Assortment of threads for decorative stitching
- Small piece of vintage or new fabric for pocket

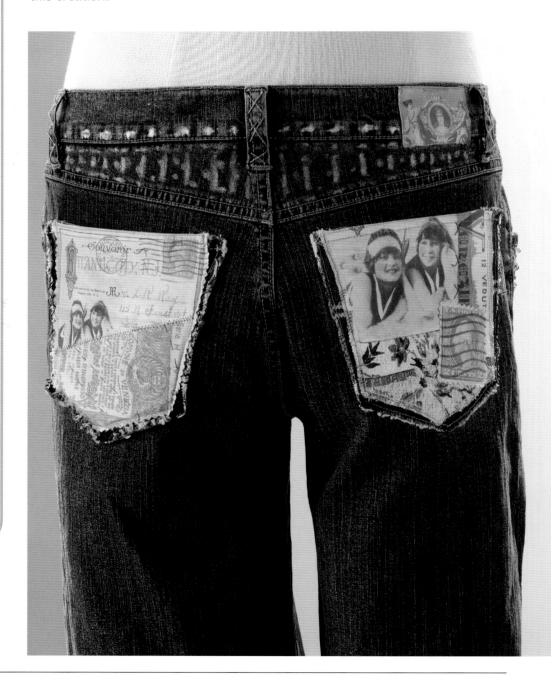

INSTRUCTIONS:

To Begin – First, cut openings for the inset images on the upper left leg. These openings need to be smaller than the images used to allow for fraying and stitching the image in place. Cut out 2 rectangles, one above the other, about 1" apart. The top opening is horizontal: 3 ½" x 1 ½". The lower opening is vertical: 2 ½" x 3 ¼". Vary these measurements accordingly if you use different images. The openings should begin about 1 ½" – 2" from the side seam. After this, wash and dry your jeans. Hem the jeans now if necessary but leave about 2" undone near the right side seam. (you will be opening up this seam). Cut out a 100 Note image printed on cotton poplin. Leave a ¼" border. Press under this border and pin the image to the right back waistband. Stitch in place close to the image edge.

Right Lower Leg – Open the right side seam from lower leg upwards about 10 ½". To apply the images, begin at hem and work upwards. Stitch the images printed on cotton poplin along the right and left edges of the seam. Align the images with the jean raw edges so they will be re-stitched into the seam. The images should be widest at the the leg bottom, then taper in as you move up to form an irregular triangle. End the images about 10" up the jean leg. Add decorative stitching at this point if desired. *(See stitch diagrams on page 127 for inspiration.)* With RST*, re-stitch the right leg along the original seamline. Finish the hem if necessary. Smooth the jean leg on your ironing board with the side seam in the center. Now add the images that overlap the side

*RST=right sides together

IMAGES USED:

- **Venezia**
- **Coliseum**
- **100 Note**
- **Ferris Wheel Horizontal**
- **Ferris Wheel 2 (larger size)**
- **Beethoven House**
- **Venice Ticket**
- **Atlantic City (2 sizes)**
- **Viterbo**
- **Albergo Luggage**
- **Foreign Currency**
- **Monsieur Paul**
- **Letter Page**
- **Report Card**
- **French Post Card**

seam. At the lower edge, you can easily sew on the overlapping image. As you move up the leg, add Lite Steam-a-Seam® to the backs of images and apply them over the seamline. Use your pinking shears around these image edges for interest. You may also use small iron-on images that have been trimmed. Iron them on randomly over the collage.

Left Thigh Insets – First, open up the side seam of the left leg about 7" or 8" beside the openings. The result is worth the effort! Cut out the images printed on cotton poplin. Center the Foreign Currency image underneath the lower opening and pin on the outside. Stitch in place, using a narrow zigzag stitch in a contrasting thread around all sides. For the upper opening, 2 images (100 Note and Coliseum) are trimmed and sewn together, then embellished with decorative stitching. Center them underneath the opening. Pin, then stitch around the edges using a zigzag stitch. With 3 strands of green embroidery floss, add a running stitch around the perimeter. Turn the jeans wrong side out and re-stitch along the original seamline.

Back Pockets – Remove the back pockets and iron flat with all the seams spread out except for the top edge seam. (Leave this hemmed.) Trace the pocket shape onto paper to make a pattern, then cut out the pattern, cutting inside the line about $\frac{3}{8}$" on the sides and lower edge only. Leave a $\frac{1}{4}$" seam allowance on the top edge. Use this pattern as a guide for your pocket embellishment.

Left Pocket – This embellishment uses the Atlantic City (small) and Venice Ticket images on cotton poplin. They are sewn together diagonally. Cover the connecting seam with decorative stitching. Cut the side and lower edges with pinking shears. Add 5 lines of running stitches across the Venice Ticket image using green cotton thread. Press the top edge under $\frac{1}{4}$". Pin this onto the denim pocket with top edges aligned. Stitch the image to the pocket close to the pinked edges.

Right Pocket – This embellishment includes the Atlantic City (large) image printed on 8" x 10" cotton poplin, a piece of vintage fabric, and a cropped section of the Venezia image on cotton poplin. The upper half of the pocket embellishment is constructed by stitching the cropped girls to the Venezia image turned on its side. Next, stitch this to a piece of vintage fabric, RST. Serge or zigzag the sides and lower edges. Sew 3 turquoise beads onto the blue ocean behind the girl. Use green embroidery floss to stitch 3 X's onto the seam connecting the girls and Venezia. Cut out the postage stamp with pinking shears and machine stitch it in place over the center seam at an angle. Press the top edge under $\frac{1}{4}$" and stitch the embellishment to the denim pocket.

Pin pockets in original position on jeans and stitch in place close to edges.

Front Pockets and Belt Loops – On all belt loops, stitch either an X or a Z pattern using 3 strands of embroidery floss in various colors. On the front pocket edges, create a wedge shape of seed stitches beginning at the top of the pocket, widening as you work out to the side seam. Use up to 5 colors of floss. On the left pocket edge, stitch 5 or 6 various beads in place randomly throughout the seed stitches. Among seed stitches on right pocket edge, apply beads more liberally and add a "string of beads" along the pocket edge. Secure this string in several areas.

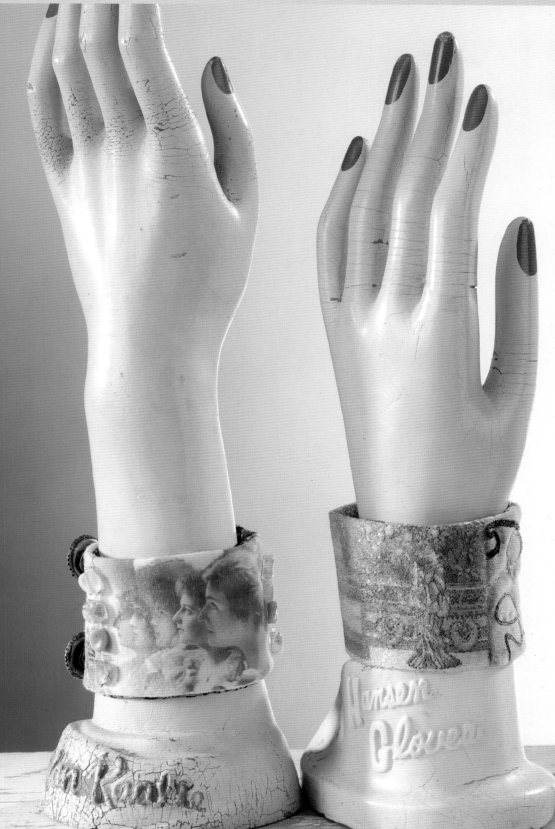

Cuff Bracelets

PRETTY GIRLS CUFF

A stunning vintage photograph of our "fore-sisters" is flanked by vintage beads recycled from earrings. Piece strips of cropped images and vintage fabrics to suit your fancy. Tiny crosses of turquoise embroidery thread descend a length of silk. Lovely vintage buttons of gold filigree look like little jewels.

COLORFUL JAPANESE CUFF

This elegant cuff is constructed with a vintage Japanese image reborn with a smattering of shimmering tiny beads. The rich velvet to each side is artfully embellished with metallic, iron-on braid. Trails of delicate hand-stitching meander beneath. Elastic loops encircle two mismatched, yet extraordinary vintage buttons to close your creation.

Pretty Girls Cuff

SUPPLIES:

- **1 sheet The Vintage Workshop Cotton Poplin**
- **Pretty Girls image (printed size approx. 3 ½" wide)**
- **Sections of images printed on fabric such as Chinese Postcard and Venezia (optional). These must be at least 2 ⅝" tall.**
- **Two ¾" vintage or new buttons**
- **One color embroidery floss**
- **¼ yard narrow black elastic cord**
- **Several assorted beads, new or recycled from vintage jewelry**
- **Fabric scrap for 9 ¼" x 2 ⅝" lining**
- **Scraps of vintage or new fabrics at least 2 ⅝" wide.**
- **Beading needle or thin sewing needle**
- **Scissors and pinking shears (optional)**
- **Embroidery needle**

INSTRUCTIONS:

1. Cut the image from fabric so that it has a ¼" border all around. Set it aside.

2. Piece assorted fabrics and/or images together into 2 sections that measure 3 ½" x 2 ⅝" and 3" x 2 ⅝". The longer section will be on the left.

3. On the right section, cut a strip of silk or other fabric about ⅝" x 2 ⅝". Pink the long edges. Place this over a seam and attach it with embroidery floss by making 6 x's down the center.

4. On each side of the image, stitch beads down the seams, beginning and ending ⅜" from the long edges to allow for seam.

5. Cut 4 lengths of elastic cord 2" long. Fold these in half to align the cut ends, forming a loop. Place the loops on the the right short end of cuff, lining up the ends with the raw edge of fabric and the loop pointing toward the center of the cuff. Place the loops slightly more than ¼" in from long side of the cuff to allow for seam allowance. Stitch across the loops to secure, close to the cut ends.

6. With RST*, pin and stitch the cuff to the lining with a ¼" seam, leaving the left short end open. Trim the corners, turn and press.

7. Fold in the open end about ⅜" and press. Stitch across the end close to the fold.

8. Try on the cuff and mark the placement of buttons beneath the loops on left end. Sew the buttons in place.

*RST=right sides together

Colorful Japanese Cuff

INSTRUCTIONS:

1. Cut out the Colorful Japanese image, adding ¼" around all edges.

2. Using 3 strands of embroidery floss, stitch a random, curving running stitch pattern on the velvet.

3. Follow manufacturer's directions and apply iron-on braid as follows: Begin with green braid and make a random, looping pattern across the velvet sections. Next, use bronze braid in another looping pattern that goes over the green. Lastly, apply the black braid over the two other braids.

4. With RST*, stitch the short ends of the image to a short end of velvet with a ¼" seam. Press.

5. Cut 4 lengths of elastic cord 2" long. Fold the loops in half to align the cut ends, forming a loop. Place the loops on the right short end of cuff, lining up the ends with the raw edge of the fabric and the loop pointing toward the center of the cuff. Place the loops slightly more than ¼" in from the long side to allow for seam allowance. Stitch across the loops to secure, close to the cut ends.

6. With RST, pin and stitch the cuff to the lining in ¼" seam, leaving the left short end open. Trim the corners, turn and press. Serge the open ends together or fold under ⅜", press and stitch to close.

7. Cut double-faced Super Tape to fit the exposed image. Following the manufacturer's directions, adhere the tape to the image. Sprinkle beads on the tape until it is completely covered. Press them in place with rolling pin or wooden dowel.

8. Try on the cuff and mark placement of buttons beneath the loops on the left end. Sew the buttons in place.

*RST=right sides together

SUPPLIES:

- 1 sheet The Vintage Workshop Cotton Poplin
- Colorful Japanese image printed on cotton poplin (3 ½" wide)
- 2 mismatched ½" – ¾" vintage or new buttons
- Black, bronze, and lime Mrs. K's iron-on braid – 1 spool of each with Teflon press cloth (included in package)
- Super Tape double-faced tape sheet
- One package Tiny Glass Marbles Crystal from Halcraft
- Small rolling pin or wooden dowel
- ¼ yard narrow black elastic cord
- Fabric scrap for 9 ½" x 2 ½" lining
- 2 sections 2 ½" x 3 ⅜" green velvet
- 3 colors embroidery floss and embroidery needle

Crazy Quilt Purse

SUPPLIES:

- **1 sheet The Vintage Workshop Linen**
- **Lady and Doves image (printed size approx. 4" x 6")**
- **1 sheet of 8 ½" x 11" paper**
- **One package Bead Soup (Vichyssoise used) or other assorted beads**
- **Beading needle and thread for beading**
- **One large button (shown is a 1 ½" rectangular shape)**
- **4" length of narrow black elastic cording**
- **4 or more colors of embroidery floss**
- **Embroidery needle**
- **⅓ yard muslin (optional)**
- **⅓ yard interlining such as fusible fleece**
- **⅓ yard fabric for lining**
- **Fabric for purse strap—3" x 44 ½"**
- **4 colors of velvet scraps (Sample uses pale pink, brown, khaki, and green)**
- **2 small pieces of brocade or decorator fabric to contrast with the velvet**
- **Sewing thread**

INSTRUCTIONS:

1. Cut 1" off across the top of the paper to make it 8 ½" x 10". From the lower 2 corners, cut out a 1 ¼" square. This will be your pattern for muslin, lining, interlining and crazy quilt.

2. Using the pattern, cut 2 muslin pieces. This will serve as the base for your purse front and back. You may choose not to use it, but for beginning crazy quilters, it may be helpful.

3. Cut out velvets and brocades to fit the pattern, allowing an extra ¼" all around for turning under or seam allowances. Remember to press all interior edges that will be on top under ¼". It is helpful to begin with a piece of velvet to cover the lower third of your bag, including the cut-out corners. Arrange more fabrics as you move up, overlapping them as desired to fill the space. *(See diagrams on page 126.)* When you have your pieces complete to cover the front, you may use these as a pattern for the back since they are identical in shape—just cut them RST*.

4. When all the pieces are in place, pin them securely and begin applying the blanket stitch around all the edges that will be visible. Make the blanket stitches ½" wide and change colors of floss occasionally for interest. Think about how they will contrast with the fabric beneath. There is no need to use blanket stitch in the center front

where the image will be. Baste pieces in that area in place with machine or by hand.

5. When the purse front and back are completed, trim away any excess fabric that extends beyond the muslin base.

6. Cut out the center image exactly at the edge. Apply Lite Steam-a-Seam® to the back according to the manufacturer's directions. Center the image on the bag front and iron it on. Attach it with a narrow appliqué stitch around the edges in a coordinating color. With a beading needle, string beads around all sides of the image, centered over the stitching. Tie off thread at one-inch intervals to secure the beads.

7. With RST, stitch front and back purse sides. Stitch the lower edge. To form the box corners, bring the side seam down to meet the lower seam and stitch across with a ¼" seam.

8. Trim ¼" from all edges of the interlining. Following the manufacturer's directions, apply it to the lining back. With RST, stitch side seams of lining, leaving a 5" opening in one side to turn. Stitch the lower seam. Form corners as you did for purse. Turn.

9. To make the straps, fold the fabric in half lengthwise, RST. Pin and stitch the long side, leaving an opening in the center to turn.

*RST=right sides together

This bag is a fantastic size for tossing across your shoulder as a unique accessory piece. It is large enough to hold your essentials, but not large enough to weigh you down. It is perfect to use when you're browsing through flea markets or galleries, site seeing, or anytime you would like to be hands-free. General instructions are given for "crazy quilting." A diagram is provided on page 126 for the piecing used on the sample and, on page 127, an illustration shows you how to do the blanket stitch. Use the piecing diagram as a guide, but have fun playing with your pieces to make this purse your own.

Turn, then slipstitch the opening closed. Baste the ends. Topstitch ¼" from both long sides. With RST, pin the raw end of the straps to the purse sides, centered over the side seams. With raw edges even, baste the strap to the purse.

10. Fold the 4" elastic cord in half, forming a loop. Baste it to the purse center back, with the raw edges even and loop flat against the purse.

11. With RST, pin and stitch the purse to the lining around the top edge. Pull the purse through the lining opening to turn. Slipstitch the opening closed. Press the top of the bag. Stitch a button to the purse center front near the top edge. Pull the elastic cord over the button to close.

Soldering Charms

The charm of any good fashion project is in the details. And these soldered jewelry pieces are loaded with charm! Follow these simple instructions to turn your ordinary project into something extraordinary. Welcome to charm school!

General Instructions for soldering glass charms:

Our method uses microscopic slides, which are readily available. *(See Resource Guide on page 127 for our source.)* Soldering irons are also easy to find at craft stores, but you should use caution when operating the irons as outlined below and follow all manufacturer's recommendations for safe handling.

Note: Remember if you are not comfortable using a soldering tool, there are alternative methods for creating glass-encased jewelry. Copper, silver, or brass foil may be used to finish the edges of a piece without solder. Pin backs can then be glued to the back of your piece. There are also several pre-made metal frames available for making image jewelry. Different types of chains are also available through craft or beading outlets.

Safety Tips: Important

Please note that the use of soldering equipment is an inherently dangerous activity and that by engaging in this hobby, you are assuming the risk of injury including, without limitation, injuries associated with exploding glass and heat burns.

- These are general safety instructions for small **lead-free** soldering projects. The process involves dangerous materials that should be kept out of the reach of children.
- Solder only in well-ventilated areas and wear glasses to protect your eyes from solder or flux spitting as it is heated.
- Use only lead-free solder. We suggest contacting a stained glass store for further safety instruction if you plan to use lead solder.
- Make sure the surface you are working on is heat resistant and fire retardant. I have found kitchen stores offer heat-resistant glass surfaces in a cutting board size. That works well.

INSTRUCTIONS:

1. Print images from CD to paper and cut out images exactly on the edge of the artwork. You will need a front and back image for each charm. Use a glue stick, to adhere the front image to the back image.

2. Clean the glass with glass cleaner and let it dry thoroughly.

3. Sandwich your design between the 2 pieces of glass. Center your sandwich on the sticky side of the copper foil tape. Wrap foil around the glass and overlap the ends. Press the sides around your charm sandwich.

SUPPLIES:

- **Inkjet paper**
- **Glue stick**
- **Glass – microscope slides or ⅛" plate glass**
- **Lead-free solder such as copper foil tape: generally ³⁄₁₆"– ⁵⁄₁₆" (width depends on the thickness of your glass or slides)**
- **Flux**
- **Jump rings**
- **Glass cleaner**
- **Paper towels**
- **Metal polish**

TOOLS:

- **Inkjet paper**
- **Soldering iron**
- **Heat-resistant surface**
- **Wooden cuticle stick**
- **Tweezers**
- **Locking tweezers**
- **Brush Q-tips**
- **X-Acto knife**
- **Scissors**
- **Jewelers third hand, or small metal clamp with protective rubber tips**

4. Burnish (flatten) the foil tape down securely on your glass with the wooden cuticle stick.

5. Use a craft knife to trim any tape that looks out of place.

6. Brush on flux all over the foil tape and let dry somewhat.

7. Clamp your charm into your jeweler's third hand or a metal clamp.

8. Using your soldering iron and following the manufacturer's instructions, cover the copper tape with solder. We suggest practicing this technique before applying it to an actual project. Solder will begin to "flow" or melt and fuse to the copper tape. It takes practice to get a smooth finish. Remember to clean the tip of your iron often with a small wet sponge. You may re-melt solder to smooth out your work.

9. With your charm clamped into your jeweler's third hand, use locking tweezers to hold your jump ring (split side down) while you dab a little solder to attach. Don't forget to flux your jump ring and the surface of the charm where you are going to attach it.

10. Clean flux off the charm using glass cleaner. Never submerge your charm in water because it is not waterproof.

11. To keep your charm shiny, polish it with a metal polish.

Alphabet Charms

The charms in this project are created with ⅛" thick plate glass, available at most hardware stores. Charms can also be created with microscope glass. Follow our **General Instructions for Soldering** on the previous page.

Remember: if you are not comfortable using a soldering tool, there are alternative methods for creating glass encased jewelry. Copper, silver, or brass foil may be used to finish the edges of a piece without solder. Pin backs can then be glued to the back of your piece. There are also several pre-made metal frames for jewelry available. Many different types of chains are also available through craft or beading outlets.

- The bracelet charms use 2 pieces ¾" x ¾", ⅛" thick glass and ⁵⁄₁₆" copper solder.

- The necklace charms use 2 pieces 1" x 1", ⅛" thick glass and ⁵⁄₁₆" copper solder.

Choose the appropriately sized Alphabet Blue/Cream image for smaller or larger charms.

Butterfly Necklace Charms

The charms in this project are created with ⅛" thick plate glass available at most hardware stores. Charms can also be created with microscope glass. Follow our **General Instructions for Soldering** and **Safety Warnings** on page 86.

Remember: if you are not comfortable using a soldering tool, there are alternative methods for creating glass encased jewelry. Copper, silver, or brass foil may be used to finish the edges of a piece without solder. Pin backs can then be glued to the back of your piece. The smaller butterfly image is encased in a pre-made metal frame. (*See Resource list on page 127.*)

- The larger pendant requires 2 pieces, 1 ½" x 2", ⅛"thick glass and ⁵⁄₁₆" copper solder. Large beads are strung on beading wire and the necklace is finished with 2 pieces of 4" wide black lace approximately 16" in length attached to each end of the beading wire for tying on to wear.

- The smaller pendant is a 1 ⅛" x 1 ½" pre-fabricated frame for encasing artwork. The pendant is strung on sheer ribbon with coordinating beads strung on the ribbon every ½" to 1".

Choose the appropriately sized Butterfly Fan image for smaller or larger charms.

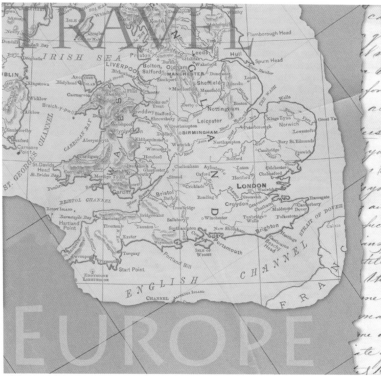

To Mr Walsh "perhaps you would not—" I have selected for you so a special, "perhaps you would "slightful" to an individual, he is distinctly an individual, he is slightly of a noble countenance by slightly light dark hair & eyes—together I think quite good—my large Italian—together I think quite good hand so—But I will hang Italian thanks to yadem andsome—But I will hang so—I am too shy so that for you to make Castonglion I will hang Italian I am too shy but

...lovely day here yesterday...
...air Victoria & I had dinner...
...Sunny—the train in which...
...telegraph Billy—I hear...
...Postal was fucked ten sea...

letter" this delig[ht] on perusing welcome missiv[e] unanswered love quotation you ever com theme pleasure then & exclaim her old frien we concest love seperated—my lov and as fervent—truly "Absence m ander" Being in

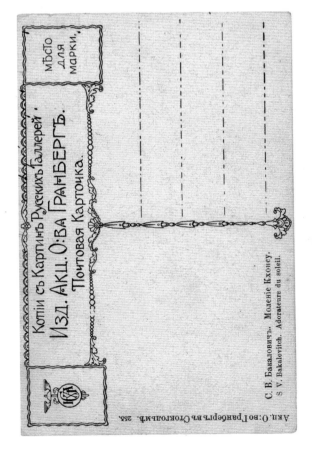

For Belt

For Belt

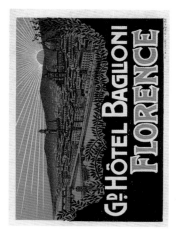

For Jeans

what similer to Mr Longacre
and I know you admire him —
by the nay "Alice" Mr L is not
married he keeps batchaloo hale
next door to the church — You
certainly must come to Ballo
this Winter and Endever to make
some conquest among the "young
devines" — That is if you have not
already placed your affections on
some one near home — or prehaps
some one has stolen your affection
from you unawars — how is it
Alice? I have not made up my
mind about returning to school —
although I think it is time I had
after haveing so much pleasure
all summer I do not feel like

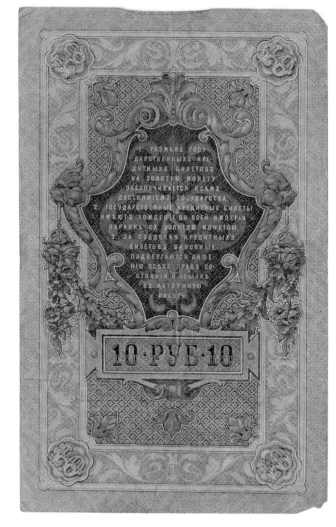

FACULTY REPORT.

CLASS *Junior* WINTER TERM, 186*5*.

Miss Alice Collinson of A. Arundel Co. Md.

STUDIES.	SCHOLARSHIP.	ATTENDANCE.
Reading	94	100
Penmanship and Drawing	96	100
Arithmetic	98	100
English Grammar	97	100
Geography	98	100
Belles-Lettres and History	95	100
Mathematics		
Natural Science	97	
Physiology		
Moral and Mental Science	98	100
Political Economy		
Greek Language		
French Language		
German Language		
Latin Language	97	100
Painting		

HEALTH.	90	DEPORTMENT.	100

☞ In this Report, one hundred expresses the highest degree of excellence in the several branches of study.

N. C. BROOKS, President.

4253. PARIS
La Grande Roue
Haute de 100 m.
Construite
pour l'Exposition
Universelle de 1900

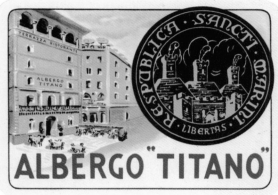

849 PARIS. — La Grande Roue, Avenue de Suffren. — LL.

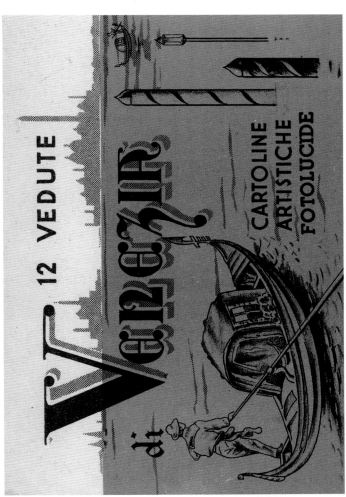

Venezia
di
12 VEDUTE
CARTOLINE
ARTISTICHE
FOTOLUCIDE

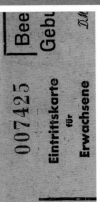

007425 | Bee
Geb
Eintrittskarte
für
Erwachsene

Serie H N. 82368

COMVNE DI VENEZIA

BIGLIETTO D'INGRESSO
AL PALAZZO DUCALE
prezzo ridotto
Lire 125.-

Il visitatore è tenuto a conservare il biglietto fino all'uscita il biglietto è valido per una sola volta e per il giorno in cui è stato acquistato presso il biglietario è ostensibile il registro dei reclami — Nessuna mancia

I.G.E. corrisposta in modo virtuale
Aut. Minist. N. 84690 del 18-2-1953
M. S. & C. - Milano

CARTE POSTALE

東京上野公方上本店験行

abcdefg
hijklmn
opqrstu
vwxyz&
12345
67890

a b c d e f g
h i j k l m n
o p q r s t u
v w x y z &
1 2 3 4 5 0
6 7 8 9 0

Holiday

Wear and share your spirit for the season.

Our holiday projects bring forth old-fashioned whimsy combined with modern trends. Do you need something to wear to a holiday party? Have fun creating your own original holiday fashion statement. And bring a special handmade project along to the party to give as a gift to the hostess. Who wouldn't treasure a charm necklace made with a retro vintage image? Or how about an angel sweatshirt to cuddle up in during cold winter months?

If you like a technique from another chapter in the book, substitute a holiday image for that special someone on your list. If you want to use our scarf pattern for a holiday version, print out appropriate seasonal images. Or use the various provided patterns that are suitable for use on fashion wearables.

Another way to extend your options is to use our alphabet that we've provided for your charms, by printing and ironing a person's name on the back of the sweatshirt. Or sew your own initials on the collars of your creations. The soldered jewelry instructions in this chapter also cross over to making your own Christmas ornaments or creating fun decorations for a Halloween feather tree.

For the Christmas and Halloween bracelets, we have provided pre-collaged images that you only need to print to duplicate the patterned effect shown.

Be sure to check your list twice because there's something for everyone.

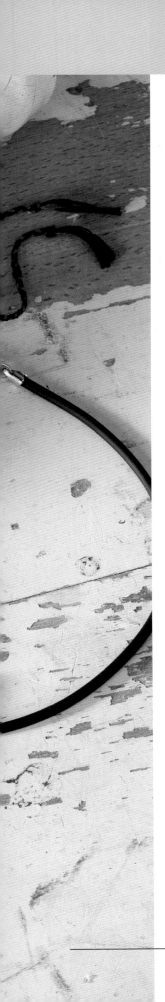

Halloween Charms

Don't be spooked by these projects. They are so easy once you get the hang of it. The charms in this chapter are a little different than the ones in Chapter 4, although you can use the same instructions and supply & tool lists on page 86.

These charms are created with ⅛" thick plate glass, available at most hardware stores. Charms can also be created using microscope glass charms. Follow our **General Instructions for Soldering** and **Safety Warnings** on page 86.

Remember: if you are not comfortable using a soldering tool, there are alternative methods for creating glass-encased jewelry. Copper, silver, or brass foil may be used to finish the edges of a piece without solder. Pin backs can then be glued to the back of your piece. Pre-made metal frames for jewelry are also readily available. *See Resource list on page 127 for details.*

- **Halloween Fairy Collage** (*photo left and center*) solder has been darkened using a black patina, available from stained glass supply outlets. The image is reversible. To make this project, you need 2 pieces of 1 ½" x 2 ⅛" glass and ⁵⁄₁₆" copper foil.

- **The Frightful Cat Necklace** (*photo right*) requires two 1 ½" x 1 ½" microscope slides finished with ³⁄₁₆" copper foil with a hanging mechanism glued to the back of the piece.

Halloween Bracelet

Here's a real treat that's better to receive than candy. Who wouldn't want a classy bracelet to wear? And they really are so easy to make. These images are set up in strips that are ready to print, cut and place.

SUPPLIES:

- **1 sheet The Vintage Workshop Iron-On Transfer II**
- **Halloween Bracelet #1 image printed on transfer sheet, approx. 9 ½" wide**
- **9" x 12" black wool felt**
- **Super Tape double-faced tape sheet**
- **DMC embroidery floss: #920 orange and black**
- **One package Tiny Glass Marbles Crystal from Halcraft**
- **Rotary cutter/ scissors**
- **Ruler**
- **Small rolling pin or 6" long ½" wooden dowel**

INSTRUCTIONS:

1. Cut out the image, leaving a ¼" – ½" white border around all edges. Cut the image size down to 1 ¼" wide. Cut the felt slightly larger. Remove the paper backing from the image and place it right side up on the felt. Follow the manufacturer's instructions and fuse the image to the felt. Wrap the bracelet around your wrist to determine its length, making sure that pumpkin is centered on top of your wrist.

2. Measure the cat, witch and moon sections in the orange squares and cut double-stick Super Tape to correspond to these dimensions. Remove the white backing from the tape and place it on top of the image. Adhere it to the tape by pressing it with the rolling pin or dowel. Remove the top protective layer of tape, revealing the sticky surface underneath. Sprinkle the film with glass beads until it is covered. Press it again with the rolling pin or dowel to firmly attach the beads to the surface.

3. Make the bracelet closure: Cut two 20" pieces of black embroidery floss, and one 20" piece of orange floss. Divide each length into 2 sections of 3 strands. Thread one length of black floss onto an embroidery needle. On the right side of the bracelet, ½" from the bottom edge and ⅛" from the right edge, poke the needle through the bracelet. Pull the floss through so 10" is on the top side and 10" is on the back side of the bracelet. Unthread the needle. Repeat with another strand of black floss ½" from the upper edge of the bracelet. Thread the orange floss through the bracelet between the 2 black strands.

4. Knot all the strands of floss together close to the end of the bracelet. Bring one set of black strands together on each side of orange. Beginning with right set of black floss, braid the strands together until the braid is 5 ¼" long. Knot the strands together again and trim the ends to about ¾". Repeat for the other end of the bracelet. To wear the bracelet, tie it onto your wrist.

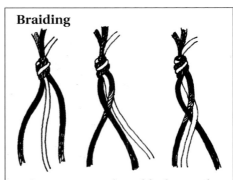

Braiding

1. One orange and two black strands knotted together.
2. Lay right black cord over orange center; lay left black cord over right one.
3. Lay orange cord over left black one.
4. Alternate right over left until braid length is complete.

Halloween Chums Pin

There's no trick to this one—it's a real treat!

INSTRUCTIONS:

1. Cut out the image only (without sentiment) leaving a ¼" border around all edges (image only is approx. 2 ⅝" x 3 ⅝"). Cut out interfacing the same size.

2. Cut a 3 ½"x 4 ½" rectangle from striped ticking fabric or print your own stripe on cotton canvas. Cut out the interfacing the same size. Cut out the sentiment, adding as much space around it as you can (at least ¼"). Press under the edges around the sentiment. Baste.

3. Center the image on the interfacing and then on top of the ticking. Add the next layer of interfacing followed by the felt backing. (**Note:** the image and the ticking are raw-edged.) With a hot, dry iron, fuse all the layers together from both the front and the back.

4. Cut a length of white rickrack about 15" long. Turn under ¼" on one end. Beginning at the center top, pin the rickrack over the edge of image all around, folding in other end and trimming any excess. Hand-stitch in place. Cut an 18" length of black rickrack and sew it around the outer edge of the ticking in same manner.

5. Place the sentiment in the center of the pin over the rickrack as shown in the photo. Pin, then hand stitch it in place.

6. Glue rolling eyeballs eyes to the faces of the cat and girl and glue the pin back in place.

SUPPLIES:

- **1 sheet The Vintage Workshop Cotton Canvas**
- **Halloween Chums image printed approx. 3 ½" x 5" on cotton canvas (this includes the sentiment)**
- **Fat quarter yellow/orange striped cotton ticking fabric or print your own using image Orange Yellow Ticking**
- **9" x 12" light orange wool felt**
- **Fast-2-Fuse™ heavyweight double-sided fusible interfacing.**
- **One package each white and black baby ⅛" rickrack**
- **One package 5mm rolling eyeballs**
- **One ½" pin back**
- **Black and white sewing thread**
- **Sewing needle**
- **Rotary cutter/scissors**
- **Tacky glue**

Halloween Sweatshirt

INSTRUCTIONS:

1. Cut the neck and sleeve ribbing off the shirt. Discard. Cut off the ribbing carefully from the bottom of shirt along the seam. Open up the bottom ribbing and press it flat. Cut ribbing in half along the center crease. You will end up with 2 lengths of ribbing about 1 ⅝" x 30" long. Straighten any uneven edges with a rotary cutter and ruler. Cut the image from the fabric backing without any border. Turn the sweatshirt wrong side out. The fleecy side is now the right side.

2. With RST*, sew the short ends of the ribbing strip together. Make gathering stitches along one long edge. Pull up the gathers. Pin the ruffle to the sleeve edge

*RST=right sides together

RST, matching seams. Machine stitch in place. Repeat for the other sleeve.

3. Turn the raw edges of the neck and bottom ½" to the outside of the shirt. Pin in place. With 3 strands of orange floss, make her-ringbone embroidery stitches along these edges, overcasting the raw edges as you go. Position the image on the shirt front center in the position desired. Pin and baste the image in place. Satin stitch around the edges of the image with orange thread.

4. Using orange thread, quilt the lines in the pumpkin, around the owl, and around the large bat using a running stitch through all thicknesses. With beading needle/thread, sew gold sequins/black seed beads to the owl eyes. Sew clear sequin/seed bead dew drops randomly at top of pumpkin. *(See sequin sewing diagram on page 127.)*

Batgirls T-shirt

INSTRUCTIONS:

1. Cut off the ribbing at the neck edge of shirt. Cut the sleeves off so that they measure 17" from shoulder seam to end. Turn ¼" of neck and sleeve edges to the outside of the shirt and press. Turn under ¼" again and pin in place. With 3 strands tan floss, make running stitches about ¹⁄₁₆" from the edge.

2. Cut out the calico print from background fabric, leaving a ¼" border all around. Repeat this for the Batgirls image. Remove the paper backings. Turn the edges under and press in place. Center the calico square on the front of the shirt about 1 ⅝" below the neck edge. Pin it in place. With 3 strands of taupe floss, attach the calico to the shirt with a running stitch around the edges.

3. Center the Batgirls image on the calico square, placing it about 1" from the upper edge of the calico. Pin it in place. Machine zigzag the image in place around the outer edges.

4. Cut the sentiment from its background fabric, leaving a ½" border. Remove the paper backing. Turn under the raw edges of the word so a ³⁄₁₆" border remains around the letters. Press. Pin the sentiment to the image at an angle as shown. Hand stitch it in place with white thread.

SUPPLIES:

Halloween Sweatshirt

- **1 sheet The Vintage Workshop Cotton Poplin**
- **Big Pumpkin image (printed size approx. 7 ½" wide)**
- **Charcoal sweatshirt**
- **DMC embroidery floss #3776 orange**
- **Orange sewing thread**
- **Beading thread/needle**
- **One package 5mm iridescent clear sequins and one package 5mm gold metallic sequins**
- **One package black and one package clear seed beads**
- **Sewing/embroidery needles**
- **Rotary cutter/scissors**
- **Ruler**

Batgirls T-shirt

- **1 sheet The Vintage Workshop Linen**
- **1 sheet The Vintage Workshop Cotton Poplin**
- **ChicWomen image printed onto linen fabric (printed size approx. 3 ¾" x 6")**
- **Vintage calico or other fabric image printed approx. 6 ½" square onto poplin**
- **Batgirls sentiment printed onto cotton poplin (3" wide)**
- **Taupe long-sleeved t-shirt**
- **DMC embroidery floss: # 3864 tan and #3790 dark taupe**
- **Tan and white thread**
- **Embroidery needle**
- **Rotary cutter/scissors**

Christmas Charms

The whole season is caught up in charm. Why not add to it with these personalized jewelry accessories?

The charms in this project are created with ⅛" thick plate glass, available at most hardware stores. Charms can also be created with microscope glass charms. Follow our **General Instructions for Soldering** and **Safety Warnings** on page 86.

Remember: if you are not comfortable using a soldering tool, there are alternative methods for creating glass-encased jewelry. Copper, silver, or brass foil may be used to finish the edges of a piece without solder. Pin backs or other jewelry hardware can then be glued to the back of your piece. Pre-made metal frames for jewelry are also available. Many different types of chains are also available through craft or beading outlets. The larger necklace has 2 charms hanging from a single clasp. The smaller necklace has a single charm hung from a sheer ribbon. Both are reversible, with images on each side of the pendants.

- **Red Candle and Retro Ornament Necklace** requires 2 pieces of ½" x 2" glass for the ornament and two ½" x 2" pieces for the candle. Each uses ⅛" thick glass and 5⁄16" copper solder.

- **Holly Necklace** requires 2 pieces of ⅛" thick glass, cut to ¾" x ¾", and 5⁄16" copper solder.

Christmas Bracelet

INSTRUCTIONS:

1. Cut out the image, leaving a ¼" – ½" white border around all edges. Cut the felt slightly larger. Remove the paper backing from the image and place it right side up on the felt. Follow the manufacturer's instructions and fuse the image to the felt.

2. With a rotary cutter and ruler, cut out the image along the red/white patterned border through all thicknesses. Wrap the image around your wrist and determine where you want to place the pattern of the bracelet. Mark where you want edges to meet and cut off any excess length so the edges meet flush on the underside of your wrist.

3. Measure the image inside the red/white border. Cut a strip of double-stick film to fit. Remove the white backing from the film and place it on top of the image. Adhere it to the film by pressing it with the rolling pin or dowel. Remove the top protective layer of film, revealing the sticky surface underneath. Sprinkle the film with glass beads until it is covered. Press it again with the rolling pin or dowel to firmly attach the beads to the surface.

4. On the right end of the bracelet, make a picot loop *(as shown in the stitch diagram on page 127)* with 3 strands of red embroidery floss. Sew a button to the opposite end of the bracelet, about ⅛" from the edge.

SUPPLIES:

FOR BRACELET

- 1 sheet The Vintage Workshop Iron-on Transfer
- Xmas Bracelet image (approx. 9 ½" wide) printed onto transfer material
- 9" x 12" white wool felt
- DMC embroidery floss: #349 Red
- ½" red shank button
- One package Tiny Glass Marbles Crystal from Halcraft
- Super Tape double-faced tape sheet
- Thread to match button
- Embroidery/sewing needles
- Rotary cutter/scissors
- Ruler
- Small rolling pin or 6" long ½" wooden dowel

Retro Christmas Tree Pin

INSTRUCTIONS:

1. Cut the tree image out of iron-on transfer, leaving a rectangular background about 3" x 4" around tree. Cut the felt and interfacing the same size as the image. Layer image on top of the non-fusible side of interfacing, then place on top of the felt so the interfacing is sandwiched between. Fuse the image to the interfacing following the manufacturer's instructions. Let it cool. Turn it over and fuse the interfacing to the felt backing.

2. Cut out the tree shape from the backing (through all thicknesses) with rotary cutter and ruler. Cut off the top star on the tree.

3. With the beading thread/needle, sew the starburst sequin/gold seed bead to the top of the tree. Sew the silver sequins/clear seed beads to the white dots on the tree. *See the stitch diagram on page 127 for sequin sewing technique.*

4. Cut an 11" strip of iron-on ribbon. Beginning at the lower right of tree, glue the ribbon all around the edge of the pin. This hides the layers on the sides and provides a finishing touch. Glue the pin back in place.

SUPPLIES:

- 1 sheet The Vintage Workshop Iron-on Transfer II

- Retro Xmas Tree image printed onto iron-on transfer

- Heavyweight single-sided fusible interfacing

- 9" x 12" light blue wool felt

- ⅝" metallic starburst sequin

- One package 5mm silver sequins

- One package clear and one package gold iridescent seed beads

- One spool Mrs. K's iron-on ribbon in white iridescent

- One 1 ½" pin back

- Beading needle

- Beading thread

- Tacky glue

- Rotary cutter

- Ruler

Let It Snow Pin

This pin has a chic feel to it and is easy to make, in spite of what seems a long material list. Imagine what a very nice touch it would make attached to the top of a present or tucked into a holiday card.

INSTRUCTIONS:

1. Cut out the image from fabric, leaving a ¼" border. Cut a piece of interfacing and a piece of white felt 2 ½" x 3", then trim ¹⁄₁₆" off all edges.

2. Press under the border around the image. Position the interfacing under the pressed edges. Turn the image over and very carefully press the edges of the image to the interfacing, taking care not to let the uncovered interfacing surface touch the iron. Center the felt backing on the wrong side and press in place. Cut a 12" length of rickrack and press one end under ¼".

3. Beginning at the lower left corner, place the turned edge of the rickrack (right side up) between the image and the felt backing where interfacing is not adhered. Glue the rickrack between the layers, pressing under the opposite end and trimming any excess. Place a heavy book on the pin until the glue dries. This will sandwich all the layers together securely.

4. Thread beading thread in the beading needle. Sew white seed beads randomly on top of the snowflakes. Following the sequin sewing diagram, sew a gold star sequin/seed bead to the top of the tree. Sew red sequin/seed bead to the bottom center of the wreath.

5. With doubled beading thread on the wrong side, bring the needle up to the right side of the pin at the bottom left corner, ¼" from the left side and ¹⁄₁₆" from the bottom edge. Take several small stitches to secure. Thread the alphabet beads onto the thread in order to spell out the sentiment, with one red seed bead between the words. Fasten off opposite end ¼" from right edge by taking several small stitches and knotting the thread on the back.

6. Glue the pin back to the back side of the pin.

SUPPLIES:

- 1 sheet The Vintage Workshop Cotton Poplin
- 2 ½" x 3" Stylish Shopper image printed onto fabric
- Fast-2-Fuse™ heavyweight double-sided fusible interfacing
- 9" x 12" white wool felt
- One package white baby ⅛" rickrack
- One ³⁄₁₆" gold star sequin
- One 5mm red metallic sequin
- One package clear, one package red, and one package gold seed beads
- One package ¼" white alphabet beads
- One 1 ½" pin back
- Rotary cutter/scissors
- Ruler
- Tacky glue
- Sewing needle
- Fine beading needle
- White beading thread

Angel Sweatshirt

- **1 sheet The Vintage Workshop Iron-On Transfer II**
- **Caroling Angels image printed onto iron-on**
- **One apple green sweatshirt**
- **DMC embroidery floss: #904 green and #349 red**
- **One package ³⁄₁₆" gold metallic star sequins**
- **One package gold metallic seed beads**
- **Embroidery needle**
- **Beading needle/thread**
- **Rotary cutter/scissors**

INSTRUCTIONS:

1. Cut out the image around the red border. Remove the paper backing, then center the image on the shirt front in the desired position. Fuse the image in place following the manufacturer's instructions.

2. With a beading thread/needle, sew star sequins with seed bead centers in a random pattern in the sky. *See stitch diagram on page 127.*

3. Using 6 strands of red embroidery floss, make a French knot berry centered on each side of the image, about ³⁄₈" from the edge. With 3 strands green floss, make a row of 4 fern stitch segments on either side of the French knot berries.

Retro Santa T-shirt

- **1 sheet The Vintage Workshop Iron-On Transfer II**
- **Retro Santa image printed onto iron-on**
- **Sleigh image printed on iron-on**
- **One red long sleeved t-shirt**
- **One ball ecru Lion Brand suede yarn**
- **DMC ecru embroidery floss**
- **One package red ³⁄₁₆" pompoms**
- **Red sewing thread**
- **Embroidery needle**
- **Large-eyed sharp darning needle**
- **Rotary cutter/scissors**

INSTRUCTIONS:

1. Cut images from background, leaving no extra borders. Remove the paper backings. Cut off ribbing from t-shirt neckline and crop sleeves to 15" long, measuring from shoulder seam to hem. With red thread, machine zigzag around all raw edges on the neck/sleeves. Turn the neck and sleeve hems in ³⁄₄" and pin in place. Baste.

2. Cut a 28" length of yarn. Thread it into the darning needle. Beginning at an inside shoulder seam, bring the needle up to the right side so the yarn is ½" from the upper edge. Do not knot the yarn on the inside—leave a floating tail about 1" long inside the shirt. Lay the yarn along the outside of the neckline ½" from the edge and pin it in place all around. When you reach the seam where you began, push the needle down in the seam and leave the excess yarn inside the shirt. Trim both tails to ½". On the outside, beginning at this seam, machine zigzag the yarn trim in place with red thread, making sure that the loose yarn tails are caught in the stitching. Repeat this technique to trim the sleeve hems.

3. Center the Santa image on the shirt front as desired. Fuse it in place following the manufacturer's instructions. Let it cool. Center the small sleigh image on the left shirt sleeve, about 1 ³⁄₄" below the shoulder seam. Fuse it in the same way.

4. Sew a red pompom to Santa's nose with red thread. Using 3 strands ecru floss, make straight stitch snowflakes randomly around Santa and the sleigh images.

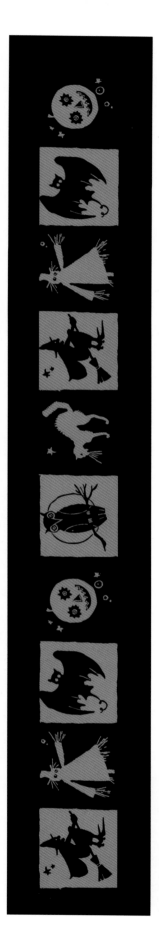

CHUMS

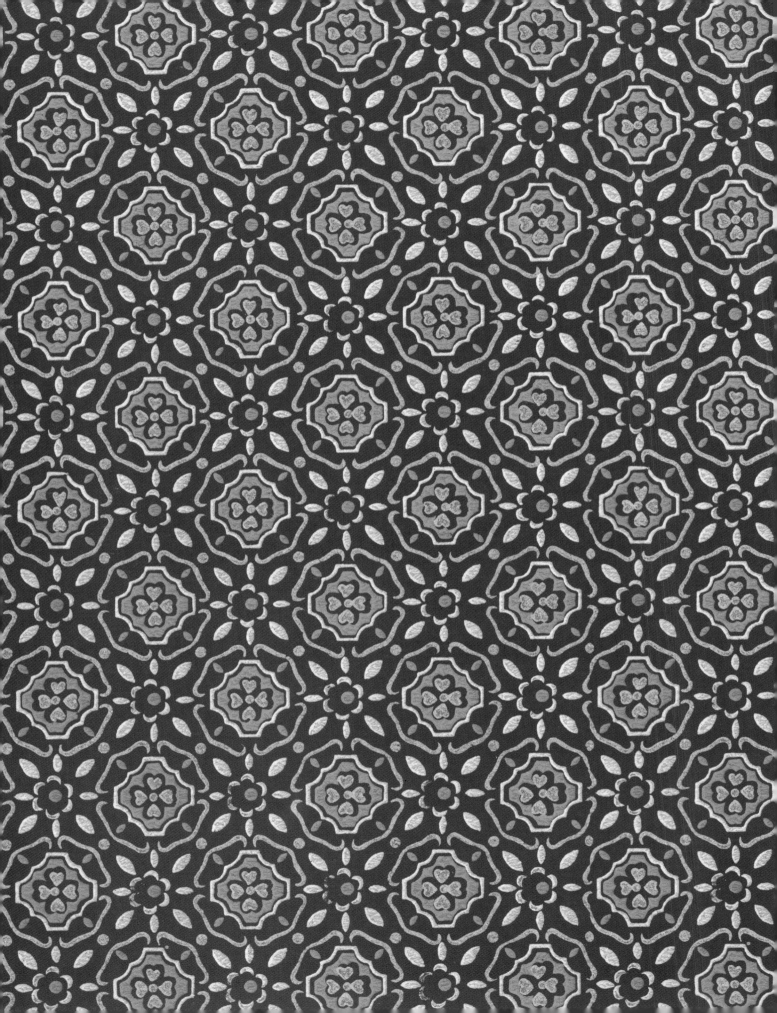

HELLO!

Creative Sources

For a list of other fine books from C&T Publishing, ask for a free catalog:

C&T Publishing, Inc.
P.O. Box 1456
Lafayette, CA 94549
(800) 284-1114
Email: ctinfo@ctpub.com
Website: www.ctpub.com

For quilting supplies:

Cotton Patch Mail Order
3405 Hall Lane, Dept. CTB
Lafayette, CA 94549
(800) 835-4418
(925) 283-7883
Email: quiltusa@yahoo.com
Website: www.quiltusa.com

SCARF *(from pages 74-75)*

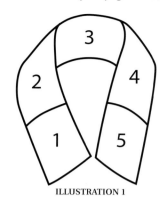

ILLUSTRATION 1

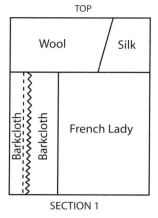

SECTION 1

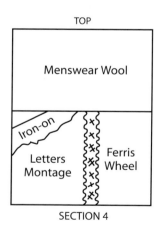

SECTION 2

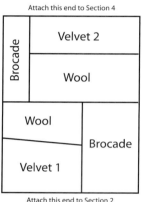

SECTION 3

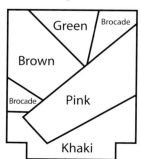

SECTION 4

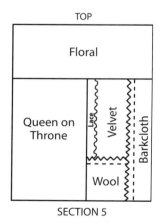

SECTION 5

CRAZY QUILT PURSE *(from pages 84-85)*

STITCH DIAGRAMS

Running Stitch
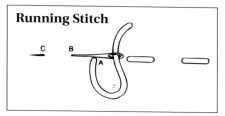

Straight Stitch
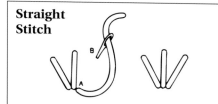

Herringbone Stitch
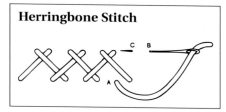

Fern Stitch
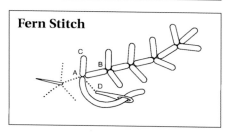

Back Stitch
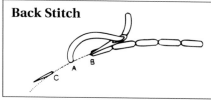

French Knot
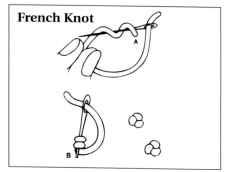

Sewing on Sequins
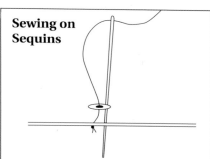

Sequins have a hole in the center. One stitch through this hole is sufficient to hold sequin in place. However, two to three stitches keeps it flat and resists loss.

Satin Stitch
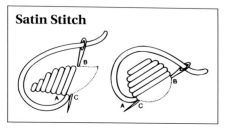

Sewing on Sequins with Seed Beads
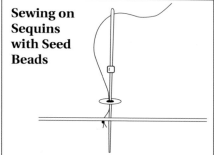

Loop one stitch through the seed bead and back through the center hole of the sequin.

Picot Loop Closure
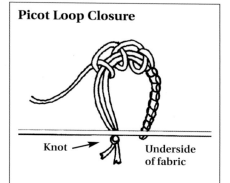

Knot → Underside of fabric

Make 2 or 3 loops the size of button, then go around the loops with a tight blanket stitch.

Sewing on Seed Beads
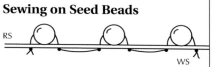

Sewing on Bugle Beads